COOKSHELF

Vegetarian

Jenny Stacey

This is a Parragon Publishing Book
This edition published in 2004

Parragon Publishing
Queen Street House
4 Queen Street
Bath BA1 1HE, UK

ISBN: 1-40544-125-9

Printed in China

Note

Cup measurements in this book are for American cups. This book also uses imperial and metric measurements.
Follow the same units of measurement throughout; do not mix metric and imperial.
All spoon measurements are level: teaspoons are assumed to be 5 ml and tablespoons are assumed to be 15 ml.
Unless otherwise stated, milk is assumed to be full-fat, eggs and individual vegetables
such as potatoes are medium, and pepper is freshly ground black pepper.

Recipes using uncooked eggs should be
avoided by infants, the elderly, pregnant women, and anyone
suffering from an illness.

Contents

Introduction

This book is designed to appeal to vegetarians, demi-vegetarians and vegans alike. Its main aim is to dispel the myth that vegetarian food is brown, stodgy and bland. When browsing through the recipes in this cookbook you will discover just how versatile, and flavoursome a vegetarian diet can be.

Fresh produce is now brought from all over the world to give us a whole array of fresh fruit and vegetables with which to work. In addition, the use of spices, fresh herbs and garlic makes for a very exciting and healthy diet.

Eating a balanced, nutritional diet is very important, and can be easily achieved by combining the recipes in this book when planning your meal, to include protein, carbohydrate, vitamins, minerals and some fats. It is very important in any diet, but especially a vegetarian diet, that a good balance is achieved and that sufficient protein is eaten.

The recipes in this book come from all over the world. There are also more traditional recipes such as 'vegetable-toad-in-the-hole', a tasty family meal in which it is guaranteed you won't miss the meat. Indeed, this can be said for all of the recipes in this book. In fact this book is the perfect way to introduce your friends to this healthy and delicious diet.

When cooking the following recipes, feel free to substitute some ingredients to suit your specific diets, for example, using soya milk in place of cow's milk. You will discover that the vegetarian diet has progressed greatly from the nut cutlet to a colourful and imaginative way of eating. Go ahead and enjoy!

THE VEGETARIAN STORE-CUPBOARD

Flour

You will need to keep a selection of flour: Selfraising and Wholemeal (Wholewheat) are the most useful. You may also like to keep some rice flour and cornflour (cornstarch) for thickening sauces and to add to cakes, biscuits and puddings. Buckwheat, chickpea (garbanzo bean) and soya flours can also be bought. These are useful for combining with other flours to add different flavours and textures.

Grains

A good variety of grains is essential. For rice, choose from long-grain, basmati, Italian arborio, short-grain, and wild rice. Look out for fragrant Thai rice, jasmine rice and combinations of different varieties to add colour and texture to your dishes. When choosing your rice, remember that brown rice is a better source of vitamin B1 and fibre.

Other grains add variety to the diet. Try to include some barley millet, bulgur wheat, polenta, oats, semolina , sago and tapioca.

Pasta

Pasta is so popular nowadays, and there are many types and shapes to choose from. Keep a good selection, such as basic lasagne sheets, tagliatelle or fettuccine (flat ribbons) and spaghetti. For a change, sample some of the many fresh pastas now available. Better still, make your own – handrolling pasta can be very satisfying, and you can buy a special machine for rolling the dough and cutting certain shapes.

Pulses (legumes)

Pulses (legumes) are a valuable source of protein, vitamins and minerals. Stock up on soya beans, haricot (navy) beans, red kidney beans, cannellini beans, chickpeas (garbanzo beans), lentils, split peas and butter beans. Buy dried pulses (legumes) for soaking and cooking yourself, or canned varieties for speed and convenience.

Spices and herbs

A good selection of spices and herbs is
important for adding variety to your cooking.
There are some good spice mixtures available
– try Cajun, Chinese five-spice, Indonesian
piri-piri and the different curry blends.
Although spices will keep well, don't leave
them in the cupboard for too long, as they
may lose some of their strength. Buy small
amounts as you need them. Fresh
herbs are preferable to dried, but it
is essential to have dried ones in
stock as a useful back-up.

Chillies

These come both fresh and
dried and in many forms. The
'hotness' varies so use with caution.
The seeds are hottest and are usually
discarded.Chilli powder should also be
used sparingly. Check whether the powder
is pure chilli or a chilli seasoning or blend,
which should be milder.

Nuts and seeds

As well as adding protein,
vitamins and useful fats to the
diet, nuts and seeds add
important flavour and texture
to vegetarian meals. Make sure
that you keep a good supply of
nuts such as hazelnuts, pine kernels
(nuts) and walnuts. Coconut is useful too.

For your seed collection, have sesame,
sunflower, pumpkin and poppy. Pumpkin
seeds in particular are a good source of zinc.

Dried fruits

Currants, raisins, sultanas (golden raisins),
dates, apples, apricots, figs, pears, peaches,
prunes, paw-paws (papayas), mangoes, figs,
bananas and pineapples can all be
purchased dried and can be used in lots of
different recipes. When buying dried fruits,
look for untreated varieties: for example,
buy figs that have not been rolled in sugar,
and choose unsulphured apricots, if they
are available.

Oils and fats

Oils are useful for adding subtle
flavourings to foods, so it is a good idea
to have a selection in your store-cupboard.
Use a light olive oil for cooking and extra-
virgin olive oil for salad dressings. Use
sunflower oil as a good general-purpose
oil. Sesame oil is wonderful in stir-fries;
hazelnut and walnut oils are superb in
salad dressings. Oils and fats add flavour
to foods, and contain the important fat-
soluble vitamins A, D, E and K. Remember
all fats and oils are high in calories, and
that oils are higher in calories than butter
or margarine.

Vinegars

Choose three or four vinegars – red or
white wine, cider, light malt, tarragon,
sherry or balsamic vinegar, to name just a
few. Each will add its own character to
your recipes.

Mustards

Mustards are made from black, brown or
white mustard seeds which are ground and
mixed with spices. Meaux mustard is made
from mixed mustard seeds and has a grainy
texture with a warm, taste. Dijon mustard,
made from husked and ground mustard
seeds,has a sharp flavour. Its versatility in
salads and with barbecues makes it ideal for
the vegetarian. German mustard is mild
and is best used in Scandinavian and
German dishes.

Bottled sauces

Soy sauce is widely used in Eastern cookery
and is made from fermented yellow soya
beans mixed with wheat, salt, yeast and
sugar. Light soy sauce tends to be rather
salty, whereas dark soy sauce tends to be
sweeter. Teriyaki sauce gives
an authentic Japanese
flavouring to stir-fries. Black
bean and yellow bean sauces add
an instant authentic Chinese flavour
to stir-fries.

5

Soups & Starters

Soup is simple to make but always produces tasty
results. There is an enormous variety of soups which
you can make with vegetables. They can be rich and
creamy, thick and chunky, light and delicate, and hot
or chilled. The vegetables are often puréed to give a
smooth consistency and thicken the soup, but you can
also purée just some of the mixture to give the soup
more texture and interest. A wide range of ingredients
can be used in addition to vegetables – pulses
(legumes), grains, noodles, cheese and yogurt are all
good candidates. It is also easy to make substitutions
when you don't have certain ingredients to hand.

Starters are an important part of any meal, setting
the scene for the remainder of the menu and
whetting the appetite. They should therefore be
colourful and full of flavour, but balance the
remainder of the meal well, not being too filling if a
heavier main course is being served, or containing
ingredients used in following courses.

With this in mind, this chapter is packed with a
range of thick and thin flavoursome soups for all
occasions and a wide range of starters from different
origins, be it Oriental, Indian or Mediterranean,
they will all make a wonderful start to a meal.

Mixed Bean Soup

Serves 4

INGREDIENTS

1 tbsp vegetable oil	1 green chilli, sliced	450 g/1 lb mixed canned beans,
1 red onion, halved and sliced	3 garlic cloves, crushed	such as red kidney, borlotti,
100 g/3½ oz/⅔ cup potato,	1 tsp ground coriander	black eye or flageolet, drained
diced	1 tsp chilli powder	salt and pepper
1 carrot, diced	1 litre/1¾ pints/4 cups	2 tbsp chopped coriander
1 leek, sliced	vegetable stock	(cilantro), to garnish

1 Heat the vegetable oil in a large saucepan and add the prepared onion, potato, carrot and leek. Sauté for about 2 minutes, stirring, until the vegetables are slightly softened.

2 Add the sliced chilli and crushed garlic and cook for a further 1 minute.

3 Stir in the ground coriander, chilli powder and the vegetable stock.

4 Bring the soup to the boil, reduce the heat and cook for 20 minutes or until the vegetables are tender.

5 Stir in the beans, season well with salt and pepper and cook for a further 10 minutes, stirring occasionally.

6 Transfer the soup to a warm tureen or individual bowls, garnish with chopped coriander (cilantro) and serve.

COOK'S TIP

Serve this soup with slices of warm corn bread or a cheese loaf.

Vegetable & Corn Chowder

Serves 4

INGREDIENTS

1 tbsp vegetable oil
1 red onion, diced
1 red (bell) pepper, diced
3 garlic cloves, crushed
1 large potato, diced
2 tbsp plain (all-purpose) flour

600 ml/1 pint/2¹/₂ cups milk
300 ml/¹/₂ pint/1¹/₄ cups
    vegetable stock
50 g/1³/₄ oz broccoli florets
300 g/10¹/₂ oz/3 cups canned
    sweetcorn in brine, drained

75 g/2³/₄ oz/³/₄ cup vegetarian
    Cheddar cheese, grated
salt and pepper
1 tbsp chopped fresh coriander
    (cilantro), to garnish

1 Heat the oil in a large saucepan and sauté the onion, (bell) pepper, garlic and potato for 2–3 minutes, stirring.

2 Stir in the flour and cook for 30 seconds. Stir in the milk and stock.

3 Add the broccoli and sweetcorn. Bring the mixture to the boil, stirring, then reduce the heat and simmer for about 20 minutes or until the vegetables are tender.

4 Stir in 50 g/1³/₄ oz/ ¹/₂ cup of the cheese until it melts.

5 Season and spoon the chowder into a warm soup tureen. Garnish with the remaining cheese and the coriander (cilantro) and serve.

COOK'S TIP

Vegetarian cheeses are made with rennets of non-animal origin, using microbial or fungal enzymes.

COOK'S TIP

Add a little double (heavy) cream to the soup after adding the milk for a really creamy flavour.

Cauliflower & Broccoli Soup with Gruyère

Serves 4

INGREDIENTS

3 tbsp vegetable oil

1 red onion, chopped

2 garlic cloves, crushed

300 g/10^1/$_2$ oz cauliflower florets

300 g/10^1/$_2$ oz broccoli florets

1 tbsp plain (all-purpose) flour

600 ml/1 pint/2^1/$_2$ cups milk

300 ml/^{1}/$_2$ pint/1^1/$_4$ cups
vegetable stock

75 g/2^3/$_4$ oz/^{3}/$_4$ cup vegetarian
Gruyère cheese, grated

pinch of paprika

150 ml/ ^{1}/$_4$ pint /^{2}/$_3$ cup single
(light) cream

paprika and vegetarian Gruyère
cheese shavings, to garnish

1 Heat the oil in a large saucepan and sauté the onion, garlic, cauliflower and broccoli for 3–4 minutes, stirring constantly. Add the flour and cook for a further 1 minute, stirring.

2 Stir in the milk and stock and bring to the boil. Reduce the heat and simmer for 20 minutes.

3 Remove about a quarter of the vegetables and set aside.

4 Put the remaining soup in a food processor and blend for 30 seconds until smooth. Transfer the soup to a clean saucepan.

5 Return the reserved vegetable pieces to the soup.

6 Stir in the grated cheese, paprika and single (light) cream and heat gently for 2–3 minutes without boiling, or until the cheese starts to melt.

7 Transfer to warm serving bowls, garnish with shavings of Gruyère and dust with paprika.

COOK'S TIP

The soup must not start to boil after the cream has been added otherwise it will curdle. Use natural (unsweetened) yogurt instead of the cream if preferred, but again do not allow to boil.

Celery, Stilton & Walnut Soup

Serves 4

INGREDIENTS

50 g/1¾ oz/4 tbsp butter
2 shallots, chopped
3 celery sticks, chopped
1 garlic clove, crushed
2 tbsp plain (all-purpose) flour

600 ml/1 pint/2½ cups
  vegetable stock
300 ml/½ pint/1¼ cups milk
150 g/5½ oz/1½ cups blue Stilton
  cheese, crumbled, plus extra to
  garnish

2 tbsp walnut halves, roughly
  chopped
150 ml/¼ pint/⅔ cup natural
  (unsweetened) yogurt
salt and pepper
chopped celery leaves, to garnish

1 Melt the butter in a
large saucepan and
sauté the shallots, celery
and garlic for 2–3 minutes,
stirring, until softened.

2 Add the flour and cook
for 30 seconds.

3 Gradually stir in the
vegetable stock and
milk and bring to the boil.

4 Reduce the heat to a
gentle simmer and add
the crumbled blue Stilton
cheese and walnut halves.
Cover and leave to simmer
for 20 minutes.

5 Stir in the natural
(unsweetened) yogurt
and heat for a further 2
minutes without boiling.

6 Season the soup, then
transfer to a warm
soup tureen or individual
serving bowls, garnish with
chopped celery leaves and
extra crumbled blue Stilton
cheese and serve at once.

COOK'S TIP

*As well as adding protein,
vitamins and useful fats to
the diet, nuts add important
flavour and texture to
vegetarian meals.*

VARIATION

*Use an alternative blue
cheese, such as Dolcelatte or
Gorgonzola, if preferred or a
strong vegetarian Cheddar
cheese, grated.*

Curried Parsnip Soup

Serves 4

| INGREDIENTS |

1 tbsp vegetable oil	2 tsp garam masala	grated rind and juice of 1 lemon
1 tbsp butter	½ tsp chilli powder	salt and pepper
1 red onion, chopped	1 tbsp plain (all-purpose) flour	lemon zest, to garnish
3 parsnips, chopped	850 ml/1½ pints/3¾ cups	
2 garlic cloves, crushed	vegetable stock	

1 Heat the oil and butter in a large saucepan until the butter has melted.

2 Add the onion, parsnips and garlic and sauté for 5–7 minutes, stirring, until the vegetables have softened.

3 Add the garam masala and chilli powder and cook for 30 seconds, stirring well.

4 Sprinkle in the flour, mixing well and cook for a further 30 seconds.

5 Stir in the stock, lemon rind and juice and bring to the boil. Reduce the heat and simmer for 20 minutes.

6 Remove some of the vegetable pieces with a slotted spoon and reserve until required. Blend the remaining soup and vegetables in a food processor for 1 minute or until smooth.

7 Return the soup to a clean saucepan and stir in the reserved vegetables. Heat the soup through for 2 minutes.

8 Season then transfer to soup bowls, garnish with grated lemon zest and serve.

VARIATION

Use 1 medium orange instead of the lemon if preferred and garnish with grated orange zest.

Jerusalem Artichoke Soup

Serves 4

INGREDIENTS

675 g/1½ lb Jerusalem
artichokes
5 tbsp orange juice
25 g/1 oz/2 tbsp butter
1 leek, chopped

1 garlic clove, crushed
300 ml/½ pint/1¼ cups
vegetable stock
150 ml/¼ pint/⅔ cup milk

2 tbsp chopped coriander
(cilantro)
150 ml/¼ pint/⅔ cup natural
(unsweetened) yogurt
grated orange rind, to garnish

1 Rinse the Jerusalem artichokes and place in a large saucepan with 2 tablespoons of the orange juice and enough water to cover. Bring to the boil, reduce the heat and cook for 20 minutes or until the artichokes are tender.

2 Drain the artichokes, reserving 425 ml/¾ pint/ 2 cups of the cooking liquid. Leave the artichokes to cool.

3 Once cooled, peel the artichokes and place in a large bowl. Mash the flesh with a potato masher.

4 Melt the butter in a large saucepan and sauté the leek and garlic for 2–3 minutes, stirring until the leek softens.

5 Stir in the artichoke flesh, the reserved cooking water, the stock, milk and remaining orange juice. Bring the soup to the boil, reduce the heat and simmer for 2–3 minutes.

6 Remove a few pieces of leek with a slotted spoon and reserve. Transfer the remainder of the soup to a food processor and

blend for 1 minute until smooth.

7 Return the soup to a clean saucepan and stir in the reserved leeks, coriander (cilantro) and yogurt.

8 Transfer to individual soup bowls, garnish with orange rind and serve.

VARIATION

If Jerusalem artichokes are unavailable, you could use sweet potatoes instead.

Red (Bell) Pepper & Chilli Soup

Serves 4

INGREDIENTS

225 g/8 oz red (bell) peppers, seeded and sliced	300 ml/½ pint/1½ cups passata (sieved tomatoes)	fresh basil sprigs, to garnish
1 onion, sliced	600 ml/1 pint/2½ cups vegetable stock	
2 garlic cloves, crushed		
1 green chilli, chopped	2 tbsp chopped basil	

1 Put the (bell) peppers in a large saucepan with the onion, garlic and chilli. Add the passata (sieved tomatoes) and vegetable stock and bring to the boil, stirring well.

2 Reduce the heat to a simmer and cook for 20 minutes or until the (bell) peppers have softened. Drain, reserving the liquid and vegetables separately.

3 Sieve the vegetables by pressing through a sieve (strainer) with the back of a spoon.

Alternatively, blend in a food processor until smooth.

4 Return the vegetable purée to a clean saucepan with the reserved cooking liquid. Add the basil and heat through until hot. Garnish the soup with fresh basil sprigs and serve.

COOK'S TIP

Basil is a useful herb to grow at home. It can be grown easily in a window box.

VARIATION

This soup is also delicious served cold with 150 ml/¼ pint/⅔ cup of natural (unsweetened) yogurt swirled into it.

Dahl Soup

Serves 4

INGREDIENTS

25 g/1 oz/2 tbsp butter
2 garlic cloves, crushed
1 onion, chopped
½ tsp turmeric
1 tsp garam masala
¼ tsp chilli powder

1 tsp ground cumin
1 kg/2 lb 4 oz canned, chopped
    tomatoes, drained
175 g/6 oz/1 cup red lentils
2 tsp lemon juice
600 ml/1 pint/2½ cups

vegetable stock
300 ml/½ pint/1¼ cups coconut milk
salt and pepper
chopped coriander (cilantro) and
    lemon slices, to garnish
naan bread, to serve

1 Melt the butter in a large saucepan and sauté the garlic and onion for 2–3 minutes, stirring. Add the spices and cook for a further 30 seconds.

2 Stir in the tomatoes, red lentils, lemon juice, vegetable stock and coconut milk and bring to the boil.

3 Reduce the heat and simmer for 25–30 minutes until the lentils are tender and cooked.

4 Season to taste and spoon the soup into a warm tureen. Garnish and serve with warm naan bread.

COOK'S TIP

You can buy cans of coconut milk from supermarkets and delicatessens. It can also be made by grating creamed coconut, which comes in the form of a solid bar, and mixing it with water.

COOK'S TIP

Add small quantities of hot water to the pan whilst the lentils are cooking if they begin to absorb too much of the liquid.

Avocado & Vegetable Soup

Serves 4

INGREDIENTS

1 large, ripe avocado	2 tomatoes, peeled and seeded	vegetable stock
2 tbsp lemon juice	1 garlic clove, crushed	150 ml/ ¼ pint/ ⅔ cup milk
1 tbsp vegetable oil	1 leek, chopped	shredded leeks, to garnish
50 g/1¾ oz/½ cup canned	1 red chilli, chopped	
sweetcorn, drained	425 ml/¾ pint/2 cups	

1 Peel and mash the avocado with a fork, stir in the lemon juice and reserve until required.

2 Heat the oil in a pan and sauté the sweetcorn, tomatoes, garlic, leek and chilli for 2–3 minutes or until the vegetables are softened.

3 Put half of the vegetable mixture in a food processor or blender with the avocado and blend until smooth. Transfer to a clean saucepan.

4 Add the stock, milk and reserved vegetables and cook gently for 3–4 minutes until hot. Garnish and serve.

COOK'S TIP

To remove the stone from an avocado, first cut the avocado in half, then holding one half in your hand, rap the stone with a knife until it is embedded in the stone, then twist the knife until the stone is dislodged.

COOK'S TIP

If serving chilled, transfer from the food processor to a bowl, stir in the stock and milk, cover and chill in the refrigerator for at least 4 hours.

Spanish Tomato Soup
with Garlic Bread Croutons

Serves 4

INGREDIENTS

4 tbsp olive oil
1 onion, chopped
3 garlic cloves, crushed
1 green (bell) pepper, chopped
1/2 tsp chilli powder
450 g/1 lb tomatoes, chopped

225 g/8 oz French or
    Italian bread, cubed
1 litre/1 3/4 pints/4 cups
    vegetable stock

GARLIC BREAD:
4 slices ciabatta or French bread
4 tbsp olive oil
2 garlic cloves, crushed
25 g/1 oz/ 1/4 cup grated
    vegetarian Cheddar
chilli powder, to garnish

1 Heat the olive oil in a large frying pan (skillet) and add the prepared onion, garlic and (bell) pepper. Sauté the vegetables for 2–3 minutes or until the onion has softened.

2 Add the chilli powder and tomatoes and cook over a medium heat until the mixture has thickened.

3 Stir in the bread cubes and stock and cook for 10–15 minutes until the soup is thick and fairly smooth.

4 To make the garlic bread, toast the bread slices under a medium grill (broiler). Drizzle the oil over the top of the bread, rub with the garlic, sprinkle with the cheese and return to the grill (broiler) for 2–3 minutes until the cheese has melted. Sprinkle with chilli powder and serve with the soup.

VARIATION

Replace the green (bell) pepper with red (bell) pepper, if you prefer.

Broad (Fava) Bean & Mint Soup

Serves 4

INGREDIENTS

2 tbsp olive oil	beans, thawed if frozen	fresh mint sprigs and yogurt,
1 red onion, chopped	850 ml/1½ pints/3¾ cups	to garnish
2 garlic cloves, crushed	vegetable stock	
2 potatoes, diced	2 tbsp freshly chopped mint	
450 g/1 lb/3 cups broad (fava)		

1 Heat the olive oil in a large saucepan and sauté the onion and garlic for 2–3 minutes until softened and transluscent

2 Add the potatoes and cook for 5 minutes, stirring well.

3 Stir in the beans and the stock, cover and simmer for 30 minutes or until the beans and potatoes are tender.

4 Remove a few vegetables with a slotted spoon and set aside

until required. Place the remainder of the soup in a food processor or blender and purée until smooth.

5 Return the soup to a clean saucepan and add the reserved vegetables and mint. Stir well and heat through gently.

6 Transfer the soup to a warm tureen or individual serving bowls. Garnish with swirls of yogurt and sprigs of fresh mint and serve immediately.

VARIATION

Use fresh coriander (cilantro) and ½ tsp ground cumin as flavourings in the soup, if you prefer.

Crispy Potato Skins

Serves 4

INGREDIENTS

4 large baking potatoes	BEAN SPROUT SALAD:	BEAN FILLING:
2 tbsp vegetable oil	50 g/1³/₄ oz/¹/₂ cup bean sprouts	100 g/3¹/₂ oz/1¹/₂ cups canned,
4 tsp salt	1 celery stick, sliced	mixed beans, drained
150 ml/¹/₄ pint/²/₃ cup soured	1 orange, peeled and segmented	1 onion, halved and sliced
cream and 2 tbsp chopped	1 red dessert (eating)	1 tomato, chopped
chives, to serve	apple, chopped	2 spring onions
snipped chives, to garnish	¹/₂ red (bell) pepper, chopped	(scallions), chopped
	1 tbsp chopped parsley	2 tsp lemon juice
	1 tbsp light soy sauce	salt and pepper
	1 tbsp clear honey	
	1 small garlic clove, crushed	

1 Scrub the potatoes and put on a baking tray (cookie sheet). Prick the potatoes all over with a fork and rub the oil and salt into the skin.

2 Cook in a preheated oven at 200°C / 400°F/Gas Mark 6 for 1 hour or until soft.

3 Cut the potatoes in half lengthwise and scoop out the flesh, leaving a 1 cm/¹/₂ inch thick shell. Put the shells, skin side uppermost, in the oven for 10 minutes until crisp.

4 Mix the ingredients for the bean sprout salad in a bowl, tossing in the soy sauce, honey and garlic to coat.

5 Mix the ingredients for the bean filling in a bowl.

6 Mix the soured cream and chives in another bowl.

7 Serve the potato skins hot, with the two salad fillings, garnished with snipped chives, and the sour cream and chive sauce.

Tomato, Olive & Mozzarella Bruschetta

Serves 4

INGREDIENTS

4 muffins	8 pitted black olives, halved	DRESSING:
4 garlic cloves, crushed	50 g/1¾ oz Mozzarella	1 tbsp olive oil
2 tbsp butter	cheese, sliced	2 tsp lemon juice
1 tbsp chopped basil	salt and pepper	1 tsp clear honey
4 large, ripe tomatoes	fresh basil leaves, to garnish	
1 tbsp tomato purée (paste)		

1 Cut the muffins in half to give eight thick pieces. Toast the muffin halves under a hot grill (broiler) for 2–3 minutes until golden.

2 Mix the garlic, butter and basil together and spread on to each muffin half.

3 Cut a cross shape at the base of each tomato. Plunge the tomatoes in a bowl of boiling water – this will make the skin easier to peel. After a few minutes, pick each tomato up with a fork and peel away the skin. Chop the tomato flesh and mix with the tomato purée (paste) and olives. Divide the mixture between the muffins.

4 Mix the dressing ingredients and drizzle over each muffin. Arrange the Mozzarella cheese on top and season.

5 Return the muffins to the grill (broiler) for 1–2 minutes until the cheese melts.

6 Garnish with fresh basil leaves and serve at once.

VARIATION

Use balsamic vinegar instead of the lemon juice for an authentic Mediterranean flavour.

Lentil Pâté

Serves 4

INGREDIENTS

1 tbsp vegetable oil, plus extra for greasing	½ tsp ground coriander	2 tbsp milk
1 onion, chopped	850 ml/1½ pints/1¼ cups vegetable stock	2 tbsp mango chutney
2 garlic cloves, crushed	175 g/6 oz/¾ cup red lentils	2 tbsp chopped parsley
1 tsp garam masala	1 small egg	plua extra to garnish
		salad leaves and warm toast, to serve

1 Heat the oil in a large saucepan and sauté the onion and garlic for 2–3 minutes, stirring. Add the spices and cook for a further 30 seconds.

2 Stir in the stock and lentils and bring the mixture to the boil. Reduce the heat and simmer for 20 minutes until the lentils are cooked and softened. Remove the pan from the heat and drain off any excess moisture.

3 Put the mixture in a food processor and add the egg, milk, mango chutney and parsley. Blend until smooth.

4 Grease and line the base of a 450 g/1 lb loaf tin (pan) and spoon the mixture into the tin (pan), levelling the surface. Cover and cook in a preheated oven at 200°C/400°F/Gas Mark 6 for 40–45 minutes or until firm to the touch.

5 Allow the pâté to cool in the tin (pan) for 20 minutes, then transfer to the refrigerator to cool completely.

6 Turn out the pâté on to a serving plate, slice and garnish with chopped parsley. Serve with salad leaves and warm toast.

VARIATION

Use other spices, such as chilli powder or Chinese five-spice powder, to flavour the pâté and add tomato relish or chilli relish instead of the mango chutney, if you prefer.

Roasted Vegetables on Muffins

Serves 4

INGREDIENTS

1 red onion, cut into eight	1 tbsp chopped thyme	SAUCE:
1 aubergine (eggplant), halved and sliced	2 tsp light brown sugar	2 tbsp butter
	4 muffins, halved	1 tbsp flour
1 yellow (bell) pepper, sliced	salt and pepper	150 ml/^{1}/$_4$ pint/^{2}/$_3$ cup milk
1 courgette (zucchini), sliced		85 ml/3 fl oz vegetable stock
4 tbsp olive oil		75 g/2^3/$_4$ oz/^{3}/$_4$ cup vegetarian Cheddar, grated
1 tbsp garlic vinegar		1 tsp wholegrain mustard
2 tbsp vermouth		3 tbsp chopped mixed herbs
2 garlic cloves, crushed		

1 Arrange the vegetables in a shallow ovenproof dish. Mix together the oil, vinegar, vermouth, garlic, thyme and sugar and pour over the vegetables. Leave to marinate for 1 hour.

2 Transfer the vegetables to a baking tray (cookie sheet). Cook in a pre-heated oven at 200°C/400°F/Gas Mark 6 for 20–25 minutes or until the vegetables have softened.

3 Meanwhile, make the sauce. Melt the butter in a small pan and add the flour. Cook for 1 minute and remove from the heat. Stir in the milk and stock and return the pan to the heat. Bring to the boil, stirring, until thickened. Stir in the cheese, mustard and mixed herbs and season well.

4 Preheat the grill (broiler) to high. Cut the muffins in half and grill for 2–3 minutes until golden brown, then remove and arrange on a serving plate.

5 Spoon the roasted vegetables on to the muffins and pour the sauce over the top. Serve immediately.

Hummus & Garlic Toasts

Serves 4

INGREDIENTS

HUMMUS:	2 garlic cloves, crushed	TOASTS:
400 g/14 oz can chickpeas (garbanzo beans)	salt and pepper	1 ciabatta loaf, sliced
juice of 1 large lemon	chopped fresh coriander (cilantro) and black olives, to garnish	2 garlic cloves, crushed
6 tbsp tahini (sesame seed paste)		1 tbsp chopped fresh coriander (cilantro)
2 tbsp olive oil		4 tbsp olive oil

1 To make the hummus, firstly drain the chickpeas (garbanzo beans), reserving a little of the liquid. Put the chickpeas (garbanzo beans) and liquid in a food processor and blend, gradually adding the reserved liquid and lemon juice. Blend well after each addition until smooth.

2 Stir in the tahini (sesame seed paste) and all but 1 teaspoon of the olive oil. Add the garlic, season to taste and blend again until smooth.

3 Spoon the hummus into a serving dish. Drizzle the remaining olive oil over the top, garnish with chopped coriander (cilantro) and olives. Leave to chill in the refrigerator whilst preparing the toasts.

4 Lay the slices of ciabatta on a grill (broiler) rack in a single layer.

5 Mix the garlic, coriander (cilantro) and olive oil together and drizzle over the bread slices. Cook under a hot grill

(broiler) for 2–3 minutes until golden brown, turning once. Serve hot with the hummus.

COOK'S TIP

Make the hummus 1 day in advance, and chill, covered, in the refrigerator until required. Garnish and serve.

Mixed Bean Pâté

Serves 4

INGREDIENTS

400 g/14 oz can mixed beans, drained	1 tbsp chopped fresh coriander (cilantro)	shredded spring onions (scallions), to garnish
2 tbsp olive oil	2 spring onions (scallions), chopped	
juice of 1 lemon		
2 garlic cloves, crushed	salt and pepper	

1 Rinse the beans thoroughly under cold running water and drain well.

2 Transfer the beans to a food processor or blender and process until smooth. Alternatively, place the beans in a bowl and mash with a fork or potato masher.

3 Add the olive oil, lemon juice, garlic, coriander (cilantro) and spring onions (scallions) and blend until fairly smooth. Season with salt and pepper to taste.

4 Transfer the pâté to a serving bowl and chill for at least 30 minutes. Garnish with shredded spring onions (scallions) and serve.

COOK'S TIP

Use canned beans which have no salt or sugar added and always rinse thoroughly before use.

COOK'S TIP

Serve the pâté with warm pitta bread or granary toast.

Vegetable Fritters with Sweet & Sour Sauce

Serves 4

INGREDIENTS

100 g/3¹/₂ oz/³/₄ cup wholemeal
   (whole wheat) flour
pinch of salt
pinch of cayenne pepper
4 tsp olive oil
12 tbsp cold water
100 g/3¹/₂ oz broccoli florets
100 g/3¹/₂ oz cauliflower florets
50 g/1³/₄ oz mangetout
   (snow peas)

1 large carrot, cut into batons
1 red (bell) pepper, sliced
2 egg whites, beaten
oil, for deep-frying

SAUCE:
150 ml/¹/₄ pint/²/₃ cup
   pineapple juice
150 ml/¹/₄ pint/²/₃ cup
   vegetable stock
2 tbsp wine vinegar
2 tbsp light brown sugar
2 tsp cornflour (cornstarch)
2 spring onions (scallions),
   chopped

1 Sieve the flour and salt into a mixing bowl and add the cayenne pepper. Make a well in the centre and gradually beat in the oil and cold water to make a smooth batter.

2 Cook the vegetables in boiling water for 5 minutes and drain well.

3 Whisk the egg whites until peaking and fold them into the flour batter.

4 Dip the vegetables into the batter, turning to coat well. Drain off any excess batter. Heat the oil for deep-frying in a deep fat fryer to 180°C/350°F or until a cube of bread browns in 30 seconds. Fry the vegetables for 1–2 minutes, in batches, until golden. Remove from the oil with a slotted spoon and drain on paper towels.

5 Place all of the sauce ingredients in a pan and bring to the boil, stirring, until thickened and clear. Serve with the fritters.

Mixed Bhajis

Serves 4

INGREDIENTS

BAHJIS:
175 g/6 oz/1¼ cups gram flour
1 tsp bicarbonate of soda
2 tsp ground coriander
1 tsp garam masala
1½ tsp turmeric
1½ tsp chilli powder

2 tbsp chopped
    coriander (cilantro)
1 small onion, halved and sliced
1 small leek, sliced
100 g/3½ oz cooked cauliflower
9-12 tbsp cold water
salt and pepper
vegetable oil, for deep-frying

SAUCE:
150 ml/¼ pint/⅔ cup natural
    (unsweetened) yogurt
2 tbsp chopped mint
½ tsp turmeric
1 garlic clove, crushed
fresh mint sprigs, to garnish

1 Sieve the flour, bicarbonate of soda and salt to taste into a mixing bowl and add the spices and fresh coriander (cilantro). Mix well until the ingredients are thoroughly combined.

2 Divide the mixture into 3 and place in separate bowls. Stir the onion into one bowl, the leek into another and the cauliflower into the third bowl. Add 3–4 tbsp of water to each bowl and mix each to form a smooth paste.

3 Heat the oil for deep frying in a deep fat fryer to 180°C/350°F or until a cube of bread browns in 30 seconds. Using 2 dessert spoons, form the mixture into rounds and cook each in the oil for 3–4 minutes until browned. Remove with a slotted spoon and drain on absorbent paper towels. Keep the bhajis warm in the oven whilst cooking the remainder.

4 Mix all of the sauce ingredients together and pour into a serving bowl. Garnish with mint sprigs and serve with the warm bhajis.

Mushroom & Garlic Soufflés

Serves 4

INGREDIENTS

50 g/1¾ oz/4 tbsp butter
75 g/2¾oz/1 cup flat
    mushrooms, chopped
2 tsp lime juice
2 garlic cloves, crushed

2 tbsp chopped marjoram
25 g/1 oz/3 tbsp plain (all-
    purpose) flour
225 ml/8 fl oz/1 cup milk

salt and pepper
2 eggs, separated

1 Lightly grease the inside of four 150 ml/ ¼ pint individual soufflé dishes with a little butter.

2 Melt 25 g/1 oz/2 tbsp of the butter in a frying pan (skillet). Add the mushrooms, lime juice and garlic and sauté for 2–3 minutes. Remove the mushroom mixture from the frying pan (skillet) with a slotted spoon and transfer to a mixing bowl. Stir in the marjoram.

3 Melt the remaining butter in a pan. Add the flour and cook for 1 minute, then remove from the heat. Stir in the milk and return to the heat. Bring to the boil, stirring until thickened.

4 Add the sauce to the mushroom mixture, mixing well and beat in the egg yolks.

5 Whisk the egg whites until peaking and fold into the mushroom mixture until fully incorporated.

6 Divide the mixture between the soufflé dishes. Place the dishes on a baking tray (cookie sheet) and cook in a preheated oven, 200°C/400°F/Gas Mark 6, for 8–10 minutes or until the soufflés have risen and are cooked through. Serve immediately.

COOK'S TIP

Insert a skewer into the centre of the soufflés to test if they are cooked through – it should come out clean. If not, cook for a few minutes longer, but do not overcook otherwise they will become rubbery.

Carrot, Fennel & Potato Medley

Serves 4

INGREDIENTS

2 tbsp olive oil
1 potato, cut into thin strips
1 fennel bulb, cut into thin strips
2 carrots, grated
1 red onion, cut into thin strips
chopped chives and fennel
   fronds, to garnish

DRESSING:
3 tbsp olive oil
1 tbsp garlic wine vinegar
1 garlic clove, crushed
1 tsp Dijon mustard
2 tsp clear honey
salt and pepper

1 Heat the olive oil in a frying pan (skillet), add the potato and fennel slices and cook for 2–3 minutes until beginning to brown. Remove from the frying pan (skillet) with a slotted spoon and drain on paper towels.

2 Arrange the carrot, red onion, potato and fennel in separate piles on a serving platter.

3 Mix the dressing ingredients together and pour over the vegetables. Toss well and sprinkle with chopped chives and fennel fronds. Serve immediately or leave in the refrigerator until required.

COOK'S TIP

Fennel is an aromatic plant which has a delicate, aniseed flavour. It can be eaten raw in salads, or boiled, braised, sautéed or grilled (broiled). For this salad, if fennel is unavailable, substitute 350 g/12 oz sliced leeks.

Onions à la Grecque

Serves 4

INGREDIENTS

450 g/1 lb shallots

3 tbsp olive oil

3 tbsp clear honey

2 tbsp garlic wine vinegar

3 tbsp dry white wine

1 tbsp tomato purée (paste)

2 celery stalks, sliced

2 tomatoes, seeded and chopped

salt and pepper

chopped celery leaves, to garnish

1 Peel the shallots. Heat the oil in a large saucepan, add the shallots and cook, stirring, for 3–5 minutes or until they begin to brown.

2 Add the honey and cook for a further 30 seconds over a high heat, then add the garlic wine vinegar and dry white wine, stirring well.

3 Stir in the tomato purée (paste), celery and tomatoes and bring the mixture to the boil. Cook over a high heat for 5–6 minutes. Season to taste and leave to cool slightly.

4 Garnish with chopped celery leaves and serve warm or cold from the refrigerator.

COOK'S TIP

This dish, served warm, would also make an ideal accompaniment to Chickpea (Garbanzo Bean) Roast (page 114).

VARIATION

Use button mushrooms instead of the shallots and fennel instead of the celery for another great starter.

Aubergine (Eggplant) Timbale

Serves 4

INGREDIENTS

1 large aubergine (eggplant)	25 g/1 oz/ ¼ cup vegetarian	SAUCE:
50 g/1¾ oz/½ cup macaroni	Cheddar, grated	4 tbsp olive oil
1 tbsp vegetable oil	1 egg, beaten	2 tbsp white wine vinegar
1 onion, chopped	225 g/8 oz/3 cups canned,	2 garlic cloves, crushed
2 garlic cloves, crushed	chopped tomatoes	3 tbsp chopped basil
2 tbsp drained canned sweetcorn	1 tbsp chopped basil	1 tbsp caster (superfine) sugar
2 tbsp frozen peas, thawed	salt and pepper	
100 g/3½ oz spinach		

1 Cut the aubergine (eggplant) lengthwise into thin strips, using a potato peeler. Place in a bowl of salted boiling water and leave to stand for 3–4 minutes. Drain well.

2 Lightly grease four 150 ml/¼ pint individual ramekin dishes and use the aubergine (eggplant) slices to line the dishes, leaving 2.5 cm/1 inch of aubergine (eggplant) overlapping.

3 Cook the pasta in a pan of boiling water for 8–10 minutes until 'al dente'. Drain. Heat the oil in a pan and sauté the onion and garlic for 2–3 minutes. Stir in the sweetcorn and peas and remove from the heat.

4 Blanch the spinach, drain well, chop and reserve. Add the pasta to the onion mixture with the cheese, egg, tomatoes and basil. Season and mix. Half-fill each ramekin with some of the pasta. Spoon the spinach on top and then the remaining pasta mixture. Fold the aubergine (eggplant) over the pasta filling to cover. Put the ramekins in a roasting tin (pan) half-filled with boiling water, cover and cook in a preheated oven, 180°C/350°F/Gas Mark 4, for 20–25 minutes or until set. Meanwhile, heat the sauce ingredients in a pan. Turn out the ramekins and serve with the sauce.

Snacks
Light Meals

*The ability to rustle up a simple snack or a quickly-
prepared light meal can be very important in our
busy lives. Sometimes we may not feel like eating a
full-scale meal but nevertheless want something
appetizing and satisfying. Or if lunch or dinner is
going to be served very late, then we may want
something to tide us over. Whether it is for a
sustaining snack to break the day, or hearty nibbles
to serve with pre-dinner drinks or as a starter, or an
informal lunch or supper party, you'll find a
mouthwatering collection of recipes in this chapter.
They cater for all tastes and times of day, and many
can be prepared ahead of time and will not detain
you in the kitchen for too long.*

*There are many easy-to-prepare dishes in this
chapter which will satisfy your hunger as well as
your taste-buds, with hardly a sandwich in sight!
You will easily find something to sustain you which
is lighter than the main meal dishes in the following
chapter, but may also be served with an
accompaniment or crisp salad, a selection of which
you will find later in the book.*

Garlic Mushrooms on Toast

Serves 4

INGREDIENTS

75 g/2³/₄ oz/6 tbsp vegetarian
  margarine
2 garlic cloves, crushed
350 g/12 oz/4 cups mixed
  mushrooms, such as open-
  cap, button, oyster and

shiitake, sliced
8 slices French bread
1 tbsp chopped parsley
salt and pepper

1 Melt the margarine in a frying pan (skillet). Add the crushed garlic and cook for 30 seconds, stirring.

2 Add the mushrooms and cook for 5 minutes, turning occasionally.

3 Toast the French bread slices under a preheated medium grill (broiler) for 2–3 minutes, turning once.

4 Transfer the toasts to a serving plate.

5 Toss the parsley into the mushrooms, mixing well, and season well with salt and pepper to taste.

6 Spoon the mushroom mixture over the bread and serve immediately.

COOK'S TIP

Store mushrooms for 24–36 hours in the refrigerator, in paper bags, as they sweat in plastic. Wild mushrooms should be washed but other varieties can simply be wiped with paper towels.

COOK'S TIP

Add seasonings, such as curry powder or chilli powder, to the mushrooms for extra flavour, if liked.

Potato, (Bell) Pepper & Mushroom Hash

Serves 4

INGREDIENTS

675 g/1½ lb potatoes, cubed
1 tbsp olive oil
2 garlic cloves, crushed
1 green (bell) pepper, cubed
1 yellow (bell) pepper, cubed
3 tomatoes, diced

75 g/2¾ oz/1 cup button
   mushrooms, halved
1 tbsp vegetarian Worcester
   sauce
2 tbsp chopped basil
salt and pepper

fresh basil sprigs, to garnish
warm, crusty bread, to serve

1 Cook the potatoes in a saucepan of boiling salted water for 7–8 minutes. Drain well and reserve.

2 Heat the oil in a large, heavy-based frying pan (skillet) and cook the potatoes for 8–10 minutes, stirring until browned.

3 Add the garlic and (bell) peppers and cook for 2–3 minutes.

4 Stir in the tomatoes and mushrooms and cook, stirring, for 5–6 minutes.

5 Stir in the vegetarian Worcester sauce and basil and season well. Garnish and serve with crusty bread.

VARIATION

This dish can also be eaten cold as a salad.

COOK'S TIP

Most brands of Worcester sauce contain anchovies so make sure you choose a vegetarian variety.

Vegetable Samosas

Makes 12

INGREDIENTS

FILLING:

2 tbsp vegetable oil
1 onion, chopped
$^{1}/_{2}$ tsp ground coriander
$^{1}/_{2}$ tsp ground cumin
pinch of turmeric
$^{1}/_{2}$ tsp ground ginger
$^{1}/_{2}$ tsp garam masala

1 garlic clove, crushed
225 g/8 oz/1$^{1}/_{2}$ cups potatoes, diced
100 g/3$^{1}/_{2}$ oz/1 cup frozen peas, thawed
150 g/5$^{1}/_{2}$ oz/2 cups spinach, chopped

PASTRY:

12 sheets filo pastry
oil, for deep-frying

1 To make the filling, heat the oil in a frying pan (skillet) and sauté the onion for 1–2 minutes, stirring until softened. Stir in all of the spices and garlic and cook for 1 minute.

2 Add the potatoes and cook over a gentle heat for 5 minutes, stirring until they begin to soften.

3 Stir in the peas and spinach and cook for a further 3–4 minutes.

4 Lay the filo pastry sheets out on a clean work surface (counter) and fold each sheet in half lengthwise.

5 Place 2 tbsp of the vegetable filling at one end of each folded pastry sheet. Fold over one corner to make a triangle. Continue folding in this way to make a triangular package and seal the edges with water.

6 Repeat with the remaining pastry and filling.

7 Heat the oil for deep-frying to 180°C/350°F or until a cube of bread browns in 30 seconds. Fry the samosas, in batches, for 1–2 minutes until golden. Drain on absorbent paper towels and keep warm whilst cooking the remainder. Serve.

Scrambled Tofu (Bean Curd) on Toast

Serves 4

INGREDIENTS

75 g/2¾ oz/6 tbsp
   vegetarian margarine
450 g/1 lb marinated,
   firm tofu (bean curd)

1 red onion, chopped
1 red (bell) pepper, chopped
4 ciabatta rolls
2 tbsp chopped mixed herbs

salt and pepper
fresh herbs, to garnish

1 Melt the margarine in a frying pan (skillet) and crumble the tofu (bean curd) into the pan.

2 Add the onion and (bell) pepper and cook for 3–4 minutes, stirring occasionally.

3 Meanwhile, slice the ciabatta rolls in half and toast under a hot grill (broiler) for about 2–3 minutes, turning once. Remove the toasts and transfer to a serving plate.

4 Add the herbs to the tofu (bean curd) mixture, combine and season.

5 Spoon the tofu (bean curd) mixture on to the toast and garnish with fresh herbs. Serve at once.

COOK'S TIP

Marinated tofu (bean curd) adds extra flavour to this dish. Smoked tofu (bean curd) could be used instead.

COOK'S TIP

Rub the cut surface of a garlic clove over the toasted ciabatta rolls for extra flavour.

Mixed Bean Pan-Fry

Serves 4

INGREDIENTS

350 g/12 oz/4 cups mixed green
    beans, such as French (green)
    and broad (fava) beans
2 tbsp vegetable oil
2 garlic cloves, crushed

1 red onion, halved and sliced
225 g/8 oz firm marinated
    tofu (bean curd), diced
1 tbsp lemon juice
1/2 tsp turmeric

1 tsp ground mixed spice
150 ml/ 1/4 pint/2/3 cup
    vegetable stock
2 tsp sesame seeds

1 Trim and chop the French (green) beans and set aside until required.

2 Heat the oil in a frying pan (skillet) and sauté the garlic and onion for 2 minutes, stirring well.

3 Add the tofu (bean curd) and cook for 2–3 minutes until just beginning to brown.

4 Add the French (green) beans and broad (fava) beans. Stir in the lemon juice, turmeric, mixed spice and vegetable stock and bring to the boil.

5 Reduce the heat and simmer for 5–7 minutes or until the beans are tender. Sprinkle with sesame seeds and serve immediately.

VARIATION

Add lime juice instead of lemon, for an alternative citrus flavour.

VARIATION

Use smoked tofu (bean curd) instead of marinated tofu (bean curd) for an alternative flavour.

Calzone with Sun-dried Tomatoes & Vegetables

Makes 4

INGREDIENTS

DOUGH:

450 g/1 lb/3¹/₂ cups strong
  white flour

2 tsp easy-blend dried yeast

1 tsp caster (superfine) sugar

150 ml/¹/₄ pint/²/₃ cup
  vegetable stock

150 ml/¹/₄ pint/ ²/₃ cup passata
  (sieved tomatoes)

beaten egg

FILLING:

1 tbsp vegetable oil

1 onion, chopped

1 garlic clove, crushed

2 tbsp chopped sun-dried
  tomatoes

100 g/3¹/₂ oz spinach, chopped

3 tbsp canned and drained
  sweetcorn

25 g/1 oz/ ¹/₄ cup French (green)

beans, cut into three

1 tbsp tomato purée (paste)

1 tbsp chopped oregano

50 g/1³/₄ oz Mozzarella
  cheese, sliced

salt and pepper

1 Sieve the flour into a bowl. Add the yeast and sugar and beat in the stock and passata (sieved tomatoes) to make a smooth dough.

2 Knead the dough on a lightly floured surface for 10 minutes, then place in a clean, lightly oiled bowl and leave to rise in a warm place for 1 hour.

3 Heat the oil in a frying pan (skillet) and sauté the onion for 2–3 minutes. Stir in the garlic, tomatoes, spinach, corn and beans and cook for 3–4 minutes. Add the tomato purée (paste) and oregano and season well.

4 Divide the risen dough into 4 equal portions and roll each on to a floured surface to form an 18 cm/7 inch circle. Spoon a quarter of the filling on to one half of each circle and top with cheese. Fold the dough over to encase the filling, sealing the edge with a fork. Glaze with beaten egg. Put the calzone on a lightly greased baking tray (cookie sheet) and cook in a preheated oven, 220°C/425°F/Gas Mark 7, for 25–30 minutes until risen and golden. Serve warm.

Vegetable Enchiladas

Serves 4

INGREDIENTS

4 flour tortillas
75 g/2³/4 oz/ ³/4 cup vegetarian
    Cheddar, grated

FILLING:
75 g/2³/4 oz spinach
2 tbsp olive oil
8 baby sweetcorn cobs, sliced
25 g/1 oz/1 tbsp frozen
    peas, thawed

1 red (bell) pepper, diced
1 carrot, diced
1 leek, sliced
2 garlic cloves, crushed
1 red chilli, chopped
salt and pepper

SAUCE:
300 ml/¹/2 pint/1¹/4 cups passata
    (sieved tomatoes)
2 shallots, chopped
1 garlic clove, crushed
300 ml/¹/2 pint/1 ¹/4 cups
    vegetable stock
1 tsp caster (superfine) sugar
1 tsp chilli powder

1 To make the filling, blanch the spinach in a pan of boiling water for 2 minutes, drain well and chop.

2 Heat the oil in a frying pan (skillet) and sauté the corn, peas, (bell) pepper, carrot, leek, garlic and chilli for 3–4 minutes, stirring briskly. Stir in the spinach and season well with salt and pepper to taste.

3 Put all of the sauce ingredients in a saucepan and bring to the boil, stirring. Cook over a high heat for 20 minutes, stirring, until thickened and reduced by a third.

4 Spoon a quarter of the filling along the centre of each tortilla. Roll the tortillas around the filling and place in an ovenproof dish, seam-side down.

5 Pour the sauce over the tortillas and sprinkle the cheese on top. Cook in a preheated oven, 180°C/350°F/Gas Mark 4, for 20 minutes or until the cheese has melted and browned. Serve immediately.

Spinach Gnocchi with Tomato & Basil Sauce

Serves 4

INGREDIENTS

450 g/1 lb baking potatoes
75 g/2¾ oz spinach
1 tsp water
25 g/1 oz/3 tbsp butter or
    vegetarian margarine
1 small egg, beaten

150 g/5½ oz/¾ cup plain
    (all-purpose) flour
fresh basil sprigs, to garnish

TOMATO SAUCE:
1 tbsp olive oil
1 shallot, chopped

1 tbsp tomato purée (paste)
225 g/8 oz can chopped
    tomatoes
2 tbsp chopped basil
85 ml/3 fl oz/6 tbsp red wine
1 tsp caster (superfine) sugar
salt and pepper

1 Cook the potatoes in their skins in a pan of boiling salted water for 20 minutes. Drain well and press through a sieve into a bowl. Cook the spinach in 1 tsp water for 5 minutes until wilted. Drain and pat dry with paper towels. Chop and stir into the potatoes.

2 Add the butter or margarine, egg and half of the flour to the spinach mixture, mixing well. Turn out on to a floured surface, gradually kneading in the remaining flour to form a soft dough. With floured hands, roll the dough into thin ropes and cut off 2 cm/¾ inch pieces. Press the centre of each dumpling with your finger, drawing it towards you to curl the sides of the gnocchi. Cover and leave to chill.

3 Heat the oil for the sauce in a pan and sauté the chopped shallots for 5 minutes. Add the tomato purée (paste), tomatoes, basil, red wine and sugar and season well. Bring to the boil and then simmer for 20 minutes.

4 Bring a pan of salted water to the boil and cook the gnocchi for 2–3 minutes or until they rise to the top of the pan. Drain well and transfer to serving dishes. Spoon the tomato sauce over the top. Garnish and serve.

Vegetable Jambalaya

Serves 4

INGREDIENTS

75 g/2³/4 oz/¹/2 cup brown rice
2 tbsp olive oil
2 garlic cloves, crushed
1 red onion, cut into eight
1 aubergine (eggplant), diced
1 green (bell) pepper, diced
50 g/1³/4 oz/¹/2 cup baby corn
   cobs, halved lengthwise

50 g/1³/4 oz/¹/2 cup frozen peas
100 g/3¹/2 oz small broccoli
   florets
150 ml/5 floz/²/3 cup
   vegetable stock
225 ml/8 fl oz can chopped
   tomatoes
1 tbsp tomato purée (paste)

1 tsp creole seasoning
¹/2 tsp chilli flakes
salt and pepper

1   Cook the rice in a saucepan of boiling water for 20 minutes or until cooked through. Drain and set aside.

2   Heat the oil in a heavy-based frying pan (skillet) and cook the garlic and onion for 2–3 minutes, stirring.

3   Add the aubergine (eggplant), (bell) pepper, corn, peas and broccoli to the pan and cook, stirring occasionally, for 2–3 minutes.

4   Stir in the vegetable stock and canned tomatoes, tomato purée (paste), creole seasoning and chilli flakes.

5   Season to taste and cook over a low heat for 15–20 minutes or until the vegetables are tender.

6   Stir the brown rice in to the vegetable mixture and cook, mixing well, for 3–4 minutes or until hot. Transfer the vegetable jambalaya to warm serving dishes and serve immediately.

COOK'S TIP

Use a mixture of rice, such as wild or red rice, for colour and texture. Cook the rice in advance for a speedier recipe.

Stuffed Mushrooms

Serves 4

INGREDIENTS

8 open-cap mushrooms	1 carrot, chopped	Cheddar cheese, grated
1 tbsp olive oil	100 g/3¹/₂ oz/1 cup wholemeal	150 ml/¹/₄ pint/²/₃ cup
1 small leek, chopped	(whole wheat) breadcrumbs	vegetable stock
1 celery stick, chopped	2 tbsp chopped basil	salt and pepper
100 g/3¹/₂ oz firm tofu (bean	1 tbsp tomato purée (paste)	green salad, to serve
curd), diced	2 tbsp pine kernels (nuts)	
1 courgette (zucchini), chopped	75 g/2³/₄ oz/³/₄ cup vegetarian	

1 Remove the stalks from the mushrooms and chop finely.

2 Heat the oil in a frying pan (skillet). Add the chopped mushroom stalks, leek, celery, tofu (bean curd), courgette (zucchini) and carrot and cook for 3–4 minutes, stirring.

3 Stir in the breadcrumbs, basil, tomato purée (paste) and pine kernels (nuts). Season with salt and pepper to taste.

4 Spoon the mixture into the mushrooms and top with the cheese.

5 Place the mushrooms in a shallow ovenproof dish and pour the vegetable stock around them.

6 Cook in a preheated oven at 220°C/425°F/Gas Mark 7 for 20 minutes or until cooked through and the cheese has melted. Remove the mushrooms from the dish and serve immediately with a green salad.

COOK'S TIP

Vary the vegetables used for flavour and colour or according to those you have available.

Vegetable Crêpes

Serves 4

INGREDIENTS

PANCAKES:

100 g/3¹/₂ oz plain
  (all-purpose) flour
pinch of salt
1 egg, beaten
300 ml/¹/₂ pint/1¹/₄ cups milk
vegetable oil, for frying

FILLING:

2 tbsp vegetable oil
1 leek, shredded
¹/₂ tsp chilli powder
¹/₂ tsp ground cumin
50 g/1³/₄ oz mangetout
  (snow peas)
100 g/3¹/₂ oz button mushrooms,
1 red (bell) pepper, sliced
25 g/1 oz/¹/₄ cup cashew nuts,
  chopped

SAUCE:

25 g/1 oz/2 tbsp vegetarian
  margarine
25 g/1 oz/3 tbsp plain
  (all-purpose) flour
150 ml/¹/₄ pint/²/₃ cup
  vegetable stock
150 ml/ ¹/₄ pint/²/₃ cup milk
1 tsp Dijon mustard
75 g/2³/₄ oz vegetarian Cheddar
  cheese, grated
2 tbsp chopped coriander (cilantro)

1 For the pancakes, sieve the flour and salt into a bowl. Beat in the egg and milk to make a batter. For the filling, heat the oil in a pan (skillet) and sauté the leek for 2–3 minutes. Add the rest of the ingredients and cook for 5 minutes, stirring. To make the sauce, melt the margarine in a pan and add the flour. Cook for 1 minute and remove from the heat.

Stir in the stock and milk and return to the heat. Bring to the boil, stirring until thick. Add the mustard, half of the cheese and the coriander (cilantro); cook for 1 minute.

2 Heat 1 tbsp of oil in a non-stick 15 cm/6 inch frying pan (skillet). Pour the oil from the pan and add an eighth of the batter, to cover the base of the pan. Cook

for 2 minutes, turn the pancake and cook the other side for 1 minute. Repeat with the remaining batter. Spoon a little of the filling along the centre of each pancake and roll up. Place in a heatproof dish and pour the sauce on top. Top with cheese and heat under a hot grill (broiler) for 3–5 minutes or until the cheese melts and turns golden.

Vegetable Pasta Nests

Serves 4

INGREDIENTS

175 g/6 oz spaghetti

1 aubergine (eggplant), halved and sliced

1 courgette (zucchini), diced

1 red (bell) pepper, seeded and chopped diagonally

6 tbsp olive oil

2 garlic cloves, crushed

50 g/1¾ oz/4 tbsp butter or vegetarian margarine, melted

15 g/½ oz/1 tbsp dry white breadcrumbs

salt and pepper

fresh parsley sprigs, to garnish

1 Bring a large saucepan of water to the boil and cook the spaghetti until 'al dente' or according to the instructions on the packet. Drain well and set aside until required.

2 Place the aubergine (eggplant), courgette (zucchini) and (bell) pepper on a baking tray (cookie sheet).

3 Mix the oil and garlic together and pour over the vegetables, tossing to coat.

4 Cook under a preheated hot grill (broiler) for about 10 minutes, turning, until tender and lightly charred. Set aside and keep warm.

5 Divide the spaghetti among 4 lightly greased Yorkshire pudding tins (pans). Using a fork, curl the spaghetti to form nests.

6 Brush the pasta nests with melted butter or margarine and sprinkle with the breadcrumbs. Bake in a preheated oven, at 200°C/400°F/ Gas Mark 6, for 15 minutes or until lightly golden. Remove the pasta nests from the tins (pans) and transfer to serving plates. Divide the grilled (broiled) vegetables between the pasta nests, season and garnish.

COOK'S TIP

'Al dente' means 'to the bite' and describes cooked pasta that is not too soft, but still has a bite to it.

Vegetable Burgers & Chips

Serves 4

INGREDIENTS

VEGETABLE BURGERS:

100 g/3¹/₂ oz spinach

1 tbsp olive oil

1 leek, chopped

2 garlic cloves, crushed

100 g/3¹/₂ oz /1¹/₂ cups
    mushrooms, chopped

300 g/10 ¹/₂ oz firm tofu (bean
    curd), chopped

1 tsp chilli powder

1 tsp curry powder

1 tbsp chopped coriander
    (cilantro)

75 g/2³/₄ oz /1¹/₂ cups fresh
    wholemeal (whole wheat)
    breadcrumbs

1 tbsp olive oil

CHIPS (FRIES):

2 large potatoes

2 tbsp flour

1 tsp chilli powder

2 tbsp olive oil

burger bap or roll
    and salad, to serve

1 To make the burgers, cook the spinach in a little water for 2 minutes. Drain thoroughly and pat dry with paper towels.

2 Heat the oil in a frying pan (skillet) and sauté the leek and garlic for 2–3 minutes. Add the remaining ingredients except for the breadcrumbs and cook for 5–7 minutes until the vegetables have softened. Toss in the spinach and cook for 1 minute.

3 Transfer the mixture to a food processor and blend for 30 seconds until almost smooth. Stir in the breadcrumbs, mixing well, and leave until cool enough to handle. Using floured hands, form the mixture into four equal-sized burgers. Leave to chill for 30 minutes.

4 To make the chips (fries), cut the potatoes into thin wedges and cook in a pan of boiling water

for 10 minutes. Drain and toss in the flour and chilli. Lay the chips on a baking tray (cookie sheet) and sprinkle with the oil. Cook in a preheated oven, 200°C/400°F/ Gas Mark 6, for 30 minutes or until golden.

5 Meanwhile, heat 1 tbsp oil in a frying pan (skillet) and cook the burgers for 8–10 minutes, turning once. Serve with salad in a bap.

Vegetable Dim Sum

Serves 4

INGREDIENTS

2 spring onions (scallions), chopped	25 g/1 oz/ $^1/_3$ cup button mushrooms, chopped	1 tsp hoi-sin sauce
25 g/1 oz green beans, chopped	25 g/1 oz/$^1/_4$ cup unsalted cashew nuts, chopped	1 tsp sesame oil
$^1/_2$ small carrot, finely chopped	1 small egg, beaten	32 wonton wrappers
1 red chilli, chopped	2 tbsp cornflour (cornstarch)	oil, for deep-frying
25 g/1 oz/ $^1/_3$ cup bean sprouts, chopped	1 tsp light soy sauce	1 tbsp sesame seeds

1 Mix all of the vegetables together in a bowl.

2 Add the nuts, egg, cornflour (cornstarch), soy sauce, hoi-sin sauce and sesame oil to the bowl, stirring to mix well.

3 Lay the wonton wrappers out on a chopping board and spoon small quantities of the mixture into the centre of each. Gather the wrapper around the filling at the top, to make little parcels, leaving the top open.

4 Heat the oil for deep-frying in a wok to 180°C/350°F or until a cube of bread browns in 30 seconds.

5 Fry the wontons, in batches, for 1–2 minutes or until golden brown. Drain on absorbent paper towels and keep warm whilst frying the remaining wontons.

6 Sprinkle the sesame seeds over the wontons. Serve the vegetable dim sum with a soy or plum dipping sauce.

COOK'S TIP

If preferred, arrange the wontons on a heatproof plate and then steam in a steamer for 5-7 minutes for a healthier cooking method.

Cheese & Garlic Mushroom Pizzas

Serves 4

INGREDIENTS

DOUGH:
450 g/1 lb/3 ¹/2 cups strong
white flour
2 tsp easy-blend yeast
2 garlic cloves, crushed
2 tbsp chopped thyme
2 tbsp olive oil
300 ml/¹/2 pint/1¹/4 cups
tepid water

TOPPING:
25 g/1 oz/2 tbsp butter or
vegetarian margarine
350 g/12 oz/5 cups mixed
mushrooms, sliced
2 garlic cloves, crushed
2 tbsp chopped parsley
2 tbsp tomato purée (paste)
6 tbsp passata (sieved tomatoes)

75 g/2³/4 oz Mozzarella cheese,
grated
salt and pepper
chopped parsley, to garnish

1 Put the flour, yeast, garlic and thyme in a bowl. Make a well in the centre and gradually stir in the oil and water. Bring together to form a soft dough.

2 Turn the dough on to a floured surface and knead for 5 minutes or until smooth. Roll into a 35 cm/14 inch round and place on a greased baking tray (cookie sheet). Leave in a warm place for 20 minutes or until the dough puffs up.

3 Meanwhile, make the topping. Melt the margarine or butter in a frying pan (skillet) and sauté the mushrooms, garlic and parsley for 5 minutes.

4 Mix the tomato purée (paste) and passata (sieved tomatoes) and spoon on to the pizza base, leaving a 1 cm/¹/2 inch edge of dough. Spoon the mushroom mixture on top. Season well and sprinkle the cheese on top. Cook the pizza in a preheated oven, 190°C/375°F/Gas Mark 5, for 20–25 minutes or until the base is crisp and the cheese has melted. Garnish with chopped parsley and serve.

Watercress & Cheese Tartlets

Makes 4

INGREDIENTS

100 g/3¹/₂ oz/³/₄ cup plain (all-purpose) flour
pinch of salt
75 g/2³/₄ oz /¹/₂ cup butter or vegetarian margarine

2–3 tbsp cold water
2 bunches watercress
2 garlic cloves, crushed
1 shallot, chopped
150 g/5¹/₂ oz vegetarian Cheddar

cheese, grated
4 tbsp natural (unsweetened) yogurt
¹/₂ tsp paprika

1 Sieve the flour into a mixing bowl and add the salt. Rub 50 g/1¾ oz/¹/₃ cup of the butter or margarine into the flour until the mixture resembles breadcrumbs.

2 Stir in the cold water to make a firm dough.

3 Roll the dough out on a floured surface and use to line four 10 cm/4 inch tartlet tins (pans). Prick the bases with a fork and leave to chill.

4 Heat the remaining butter or margarine in a frying pan (skillet). Discard the stems from the watercress and add to the pan with the garlic and shallot, cooking for 1–2 minutes until the watercress is wilted.

5 Remove the pan from the heat and stir in the cheese, yogurt and paprika.

6 Spoon the mixture into the pastry cases and cook in a preheated oven, 180°C/350°F/Gas Mark 4, for 20 minutes or until the

filling is firm. Turn out the tartlets and serve.

VARIATION

Use spinach instead of the watercress, making sure it is well drained before mixing with the remaining filling ingredients.

Vegetable-Filled Ravioli

Serves 4

INGREDIENTS

FILLING:
25 g/1 oz/3 tbsp butter or
    vegetarian margarine
2 garlic cloves, crushed
1 small leek, chopped
2 celery sticks, chopped

200 g/7 oz/2¹⁄₃ cups open-cap
    mushrooms, chopped
1 egg, beaten
2 tbsp grated vegetarian Parmesan
    cheese
salt and pepper

RAVIOLI:
4 sheets filo pastry
25 g/1 oz/3 tbsp vegetarian
    margarine
oil, for deep-frying

1 To make the filling, melt the butter or margarine in a frying pan (skillet) and sauté the garlic and leek for 2–3 minutes until softened.

2 Add the celery and mushrooms and cook for a further 4–5 minutes until all of the vegetables are tender.

3 Turn off the heat and stir in the egg and grated Parmesan cheese. Season with salt and pepper to taste.

4 Lay the pastry sheets on a chopping board and cut each into nine squares.

5 Spoon a little of the filling into the centre half of the squares and brush the edges of the pastry with butter or margarine. Lay another square on top and seal the edges to make a parcel.

6 Heat the oil for deep-frying to 180°C/350°F or until a cube of bread browns in 30 seconds. Fry the ravioli, in batches, for 2–3 minutes or until golden brown. Remove from the oil with a slotted spoon and pat dry on absorbent paper towels. Transfer to a warm serving plate and serve.

COOK'S TIP

Parmesan cheese is generally non-vegetarian, however, there is an Italian Parmesan called Grano Padano, which is usually vegetarian. Alternatively you could use Pecorino.

Bulgur-Filled Aubergines (Eggplants)

Serves 4

INGREDIENTS

4 medium aubergines (eggplants)	2 tbsp pine kernels (nuts)	50 g/1³/4 oz/³/4 cup button
salt	¹/2 tsp turmeric	mushrooms, chopped
175 g/6 oz/³/4 cup bulgur wheat	1 tsp chilli powder	2 tbsp raisins
300 ml/¹/2 pint/1¹/4 cups	2 celery sticks, chopped	2 tbsp chopped fresh coriander
boiling water	4 spring onions (scallions),	(cilantro)
3 tbsp olive oil	chopped	green salad, to serve
2 garlic cloves, crushed	1 carrot, grated	

1 Cut the aubergines (eggplants) in half lengthwise and scoop out the flesh with a teaspoon. Chop the flesh and set aside. Rub the insides of the aubergines (eggplants) with a little salt and leave to stand for 20 minutes.

2 Meanwhile, put the bulgur wheat in a mixing bowl and pour the boiling water over the top. Leave to stand for 20 minutes or until the water has been absorbed.

3 Heat the oil in a frying pan (skillet). Add the garlic, pine kernels (nuts), turmeric, chilli powder, celery, spring onions (scallions), carrot, mushrooms and raisins and cook for 2–3 minutes.

4 Stir in the reserved aubergine (eggplant) flesh and cook for a further 2–3 minutes. Add the coriander (cilantro), mixing well.

5 Remove the pan from the heat and stir in the bulgur wheat. Rinse the aubergine (eggplant) shells under cold water and pat dry with paper towels.

6 Spoon the bulgur filling into the aubergines (eggplants) and place in a roasting tin (pan). Pour in a little boiling water and cook in a preheated oven, 180°C/350°F/Gas Mark 4, for 15–20 minutes.

7 Serve hot with a green salad.

Lentil Croquettes

Serves 4

INGREDIENTS

225 g/8 oz/1 ¼ cups split red lentils	½ tsp chilli powder	1 tsp turmeric
1 green (bell) pepper, finely chopped	1 tsp ground cumin	1 tsp chilli powder
1 red onion, finely chopped	2 tsp lemon juice	4 tbsp vegetable oil
2 garlic cloves, crushed	2 tbsp chopped unsalted peanuts	salt and pepper
1 tsp garam masala	600 ml/1 pint/2½ cups water	salad leaves and fresh herbs, to serve
	1 egg, beaten	
	3 tbsp plain (all-purpose) flour	

1 Put the lentils in a large saucepan with the (bell) pepper, onion, garlic, garam masala, chilli powder, ground cumin, lemon juice and peanuts.

2 Add the water and bring to the boil. Reduce the heat and simmer for 30 minutes or until the liquid has been absorbed, stirring occasionally.

3 Remove the mixture from the heat and leave to cool slightly. Beat

in the egg and season with salt and pepper to taste. Leave to cool completely.

4 With floured hands, form the mixture into eight oblong shapes.

5 Mix the flour, turmeric and chilli powder together on a small plate. Roll the croquettes in the spiced flour mixture to coat.

6 Heat the oil in a large frying pan (skillet) and cook the croquettes, in

batches, for 10 minutes, turning once, until crisp on both sides. Serve the croquettes with salad leaves and fresh herbs.

COOK'S TIP

Other lentils could be used, but they will require soaking and precooking before use. Red lentils are used for speed and convenience.

Refried Beans with Tortillas

Serves 4

INGREDIENTS

BEANS:

2 tbsp olive oil

1 onion, finely chopped

3 garlic cloves, crushed

1 green chilli, chopped

400 g/14 oz can red kidney
    beans, drained

400 g/14 oz can pinto
    beans, drained

2 tbsp chopped coriander
    (cilantro)

150 ml/¼ pint/⅔ cup
    vegetable stock

8 wheat tortillas

25 g/1 oz/ ¼ cup vegetarian
    Cheddar cheese, grated

salt and pepper

RELISH:

4 spring onions (scallions),
    chopped

1 red onion, chopped

1 green chilli, chopped

1 tbsp garlic wine vinegar

1 tsp caster (superfine) sugar

1 tomato, chopped

1 Heat the oil for the beans in a large frying pan (skillet). Add the onion and sauté for 3–5 minutes. Add the garlic and chilli and cook for 1 minute.

2 Mash the beans with a potato masher and stir into the pan with the coriander (cilantro).

3 Stir in the stock and cook the beans, stirring, for 5 minutes until soft and pulpy.

4 Place the tortillas on a baking tray (cookie sheet) and heat through in a warm oven for 1–2 minutes.

5 Mix the relish ingredients together.

6 Spoon the beans into a serving dish and top with the cheese. Season well. Roll the tortillas and serve with the relish and beans.

COOK'S TIP

Add a little more liquid to the beans when they are cooking if they begin to catch on the bottom of the frying pan (skillet).

Brown Rice, Vegetable & Herb Gratin

Serves 4

INGREDIENTS

100 g/3½ oz/⅓ cup brown rice	1 courgette (zucchini), sliced	100 g/3½ oz/1 cup grated
2 tbsp butter or margarine	75 g/2¾ oz baby corn cobs,	Mozzarella cheese
1 red onion, chopped	halved lengthwise	2 tbsp wholemeal (whole wheat)
2 garlic cloves, crushed	2 tbsp sunflower seeds	breadcrumbs
1 carrot, cut into matchsticks	3 tbsp chopped mixed herbs	salt and pepper

1 Cook the rice in a saucepan of boiling salted water for 20 minutes. Drain well.

2 Lightly grease a 900 ml / 1½ pint ovenproof dish.

3 Heat the butter in a frying pan (skillet). Add the onion and cook, stirring, for 2 minutes or until softened.

4 Add the garlic, carrot, courgette (zucchini) and corn cobs and cook for a further 5 minutes, stirring.

5 Mix the rice with the sunflower seeds and mixed herbs and stir into the pan.

6 Stir in half of the Mozzarella cheese and season with salt and pepper to taste.

7 Spoon the mixture into the greased dish and top with the breadcrumbs and remaining cheese.

Cook in a preheated oven, 180°C/350°F/Gas Mark 4, for 25–30 minutes or until the cheese begins to turn golden. Serve.

VARIATION

Use an alternative rice, such as basmati, and flavour the dish with curry spices, if you prefer.

Green Lentil & Mixed Vegetable Pan-fry

Serves 4

INGREDIENTS

150 g/5¹/₂ oz/3³/₄ cups
   green lentils
4 tbsp butter or vegetarian
   margarine
2 garlic cloves, crushed
2 tbsp olive oil
1 tbsp cider vinegar

1 red onion, cut into eight
50 g/1³/₄ oz baby corn cobs,
   halved lengthwise
1 yellow (bell) pepper, cut into
   strips
1 red (bell) pepper, cut into strips
50 g/1³/₄ oz French (green)

beans, halved
125 ml/4 fl oz/6 tbsp /¹/₂ cup
   vegetable stock
2 tbsp clear honey
salt and pepper
crusty bread, to serve

1 Soak the lentils in a large saucepan of cold water for 25 minutes. Bring to the boil, reduce the heat and simmer for 20 minutes. Drain thoroughly.

2 Add 1 tablespoon of the butter or margarine, 1 garlic clove, 1 tablespoon of oil and the vinegar to the lentils and mix well.

3 Melt the remaining butter, garlic and oil in a frying pan (skillet) and stir-fry the onion, corn cobs, (bell) peppers and beans for 3–4 minutes.

4 Add the vegetable stock and bring to the boil for about 10 minutes or until the liquid has evaporated.

5 Add the honey and season with salt and pepper to taste. Stir in the lentil mixture and cook for 1 minute to heat through. Spoon on to warmed serving plates and serve with crusty bread.

VARIATION

This pan-fry is very versatile – you can use a mixture of your favourite vegetables, if you prefer. Try courgettes (zucchini), carrots or mangetout (snow peas).

Falafel

Serves 4

INGREDIENTS

650 g/1 lb 7 oz/6 cups canned chickpeas (garbanzo beans), drained	2 small red chillies	100 g/3½ oz/1 cup wholemeal (whole wheat) breadcrumbs
1 red onion, chopped	1 tsp ground cumin	vegetable oil, for deep-frying
3 garlic cloves, crushed	1 tsp ground coriander	salt and pepper
100 g/3½ oz wholemeal (whole wheat) bread	½ tsp turmeric	tomato and cucumber salad and lemon wedges, to serve
	1 tbsp chopped coriander (cilantro), plus extra to garnish	
	1 egg, beaten	

1 Put the chickpeas (garbanzo beans), onion, garlic, bread, chillies, spices and coriander (cilantro) in a food processor and blend for 30 seconds. Stir and season well.

2 Remove the mixture from the food processor and shape into walnut-sized balls.

3 Place the beaten egg in a shallow bowl and place the wholemeal

(wholewheat) breadcrumbs on a plate. Dip the balls into the egg to coat and then roll them in the breadcrumbs, shaking off any excess.

4 Heat the oil for deep-frying to 180°C/350°F or until a cube of bread browns in 30 seconds. Fry the falafel, in batches, for 2–3 minutes until crisp and browned. Remove from the oil with a slotted spoon and dry on absorbent paper towels. Garnish with

coriander (cilantro) and serve with a tomato and cucumber salad and lemon wedges.

COOK'S TIP

Serve the falafel with a coriander (cilantro) and yogurt sauce. Mix 150 ml/¼ pint/⅔ cup natural (unsweetened) yogurt with 2 tbsp chopped coriander (cilantro) and 1 crushed garlic clove.

Cabbage & Walnut Stir-Fry

Serves 4

INGREDIENTS

350 g/12 oz white cabbage
350 g/12 oz red cabbage
4 tbsp peanut oil
1 tbsp walnut oil
2 garlic cloves, crushed

8 spring onions (scallions),
　trimmed
225 g/8 oz firm tofu (bean curd),
　cubed
2 tbsp lemon juice

100 g/3½ oz walnut halves
2 tsp Dijon mustard
2 tsp poppy seeds
salt and pepper

1 Using a sharp knife, shred the white and red cabbages thinly and set aside until required.

2 Heat the peanut and walnut oils in a preheated wok. Add the garlic, cabbage, spring onions (scallions) and tofu (bean curd) and cook for 5 minutes, stirring.

3 Add the lemon juice, walnuts and mustard, season with salt and pepper and cook for a further 5 minutes or until the cabbage is tender.

4 Transfer the stir-fry to a warm serving bowl, sprinkle with poppy seeds and serve.

COOK'S TIP

As well as adding protein, vitamins and useful fats to the diet, nuts and seeds add flavour and texture to vegetarian meals. Keep a good supply of them in your store-cupboard as they can be used in a great variety of dishes – salads, bakes, stir-fries to name but a few.

VARIATION

Sesame seeds could be used instead of the poppy seeds and drizzle 1 teaspoon of sesame oil over the dish just before serving, if you wish.

Spinach Frittata

Serves 4

INGREDIENTS

450 g/1 lb spinach

2 tsp water

4 eggs, beaten

2 tbsp single (light) cream

2 garlic cloves, crushed

50 g/1¾ oz/¾ cup canned
sweetcorn, drained

1 celery stick, chopped

1 red chilli, chopped

2 tomatoes, seeded and diced

2 tbsp olive oil

2 tbsp butter

25 g/1 oz/¼ cup pecan
nut halves

2 tbsp grated Pecorino cheese

25 g/1 oz/¼ cup Fontina
cheese, cubed

a pinch of paprika

1 Cook the spinach in 2 teaspoons of water in a covered pan for 5 minutes. Drain thoroughly and pat dry on absorbent paper towels.

2 Beat the eggs in a bowl and stir in the spinach, single (light) cream, garlic, sweetcorn, celery, chilli and tomatoes until the ingredients are well mixed.

3 Heat the oil and butter in a 20 cm/8 inch heavy-based frying pan (skillet).

4 Spoon the egg mixture into the frying pan (skillet) and sprinkle with the pecan nut halves, Pecorino and Fontina cheeses and paprika. Cook without stirring over a medium heat for 5–7 minutes or until the underside of the frittata is brown.

5 Put a large plate over the pan and invert to turn out the frittata. Slide it back into the frying pan (skillet) and cook the other side for a further 2–3 minutes. Serve the frittata straight from the frying pan (skillet) or transfer to a serving plate.

Marinated Grilled (Broiled) Fennel

Serves 4

INGREDIENTS

2 fennel bulbs
1 red (bell) pepper, cut into large
    cubes
1 lime, cut into eight wedges

MARINADE:
2 tbsp lime juice
4 tbsp olive oil
2 garlic cloves, crushed
1 tsp wholegrain mustard

1 tbsp chopped thyme
fennel fronds, to garnish
crisp salad, to serve

1 Cut each of the fennel bulbs into eight pieces and place in a shallow dish. Mix in the (bell) peppers.

2 To make the marinade, combine the lime juice, oil, garlic, mustard and thyme. Pour the marinade over the fennel and (bell) peppers and leave to marinate for 1 hour.

3 Thread the fennel and (bell) peppers on to wooden skewers with the lime wedges. Preheat a grill (broiler) to medium and grill (broil) the kebabs (kabobs) for 10 minutes, turning and basting with the marinade.

4 Transfer to serving plates, garnish with fennel fronds and serve with a crisp salad.

VARIATION

Substitute 2 tbsp orange juice for the lime juice and add 1 tbsp honey, if you prefer.

COOK'S TIP

Soak the skewers in water for 20 minutes before using to prevent them from burning during cooking.

Ciabatta Rolls

Serves 4

INGREDIENTS

4 ciabatta rolls
2 tbsp olive oil
1 garlic clove crushed

FILLING:
1 red (bell) pepper
1 green (bell) pepper
1 yellow (bell) pepper
4 radishes, sliced

1 bunch watercress
100 g/3½ oz/8 tbsp cream
cheese

1 Slice the ciabatta rolls in half. Heat the olive oil and crushed garlic in a saucepan. Pour the garlic and oil mixture over the cut surfaces of the rolls and leave to stand.

2 Halve the (bell) peppers and place, skin side uppermost, on a grill (broiler) rack. Cook under a hot grill (broiler) for 8–10 minutes until just beginning to char. Remove the (bell) peppers from the grill (broiler), peel and slice thinly.

3 Arrange the radish slices on one half of each roll with a few watercress leaves. Spoon the cream cheese on top. Pile the (bell) peppers on top of the cream cheese and top with the other half of the roll. Serve.

COOK'S TIP

To peel (bell) peppers, wrap them in foil after grilling (broiling). This traps the steam, loosening the skins and making them easier to peel.

COOK'S TIP

Allow the (bell) peppers to cool slightly before filling the roll otherwise the cheese will melt.

Main Meals

This is the most comprehensive chapter in the book, being perhaps the most important. In a vegetarian diet it is essential to eat a good balance of foods and the following recipes make good use of pulses (legumes), grains, tofu (bean curd) and vegetables to aid in this quest. The recipes in this chapter will enable you to build a balanced, nutritious and flavourful menu which will meet all of your needs.

Anyone who ever thought that vegetarian meals were dull will be proved wrong by the rich variety of dishes in this chapter. You'll recognize influences from Indian, Mexican and Chinese cooking, but there are also traditional stews and casseroles as well as hearty bakes and roasts. They all make exciting eating at any time of year, at virtually any occasion. There are ideas for mid-week meals or for entertaining, some traditional and some more unusual. Don't be afraid to substitute ingredients where appropriate. There is no reason why you cannot enjoy experimenting and adding your own touch to these imaginative ideas.

Mushroom & Spinach Puff Pastry

Serves 4

INGREDIENTS

2 tbsp butter	175 g/6 oz baby spinach	salt and pepper
1 red onion, halved and sliced	pinch of nutmeg	2 tsp poppy seeds
2 garlic cloves, crushed	4 tbsp double (heavy) cream	
225 g/8 oz/3 cups open-cap mushrooms, sliced	225 g/8 oz prepared puff pastry	
	1 egg, beaten	

1 Melt the butter in a frying pan (skillet). Add the onion and garlic to the pan and sauté for 3–4 minutes, stirring well, until the onion has softened.

2 Add the mushrooms, spinach and nutmeg and cook for a further 2–3 minutes.

3 Stir in the double (heavy) cream, mixing well.

4 Season with salt and pepper to taste and remove the pan from the heat.

5 Roll the pastry out on a lightly floured surface and cut into four 15 cm/6 inch circles.

6 Spoon a quarter of the filling on to one half of each circle and fold the pastry over to encase the filling. Press down to seal the edges of the pastry and brush with the beaten egg. Sprinkle with the poppy seeds.

7 Place the parcels on to a dampened baking tray (cookie sheet) and cook in a preheated oven, 200°C/400°F/Gas Mark 6, for 20 minutes until risen and golden brown.

8 Transfer the mushroom and spinach puff pastry parcels to serving plates and serve immediately.

Chickpea (Garbanzo Bean) Roast with Sherry Sauce

Serves 4

INGREDIENTS

450 g/1 lb can chickpeas
   (garbanzo beans), drained
1 tsp marmite (yeast extract)
150 g/5¹/₂ oz/1¹/₄ cups chopped
   walnuts
150 g/5¹/₂ oz/1¹/₄ cups fresh
   white breadcrumbs
1 onion, finely chopped
100 g/3¹/₂ oz/1¹/₄ cups

mushrooms, sliced
50 g/1³/₄ oz canned sweetcorn,
   drained
2 garlic cloves, crushed
2 tbsp dry sherry
2 tbsp vegetable stock
1 tbsp chopped coriander
   (cilantro)
225 g/8 oz prepared puff pastry

1 egg, beaten
2 tbsp milk
salt and pepper
SAUCE:
1 tbsp vegetable oil
1 leek, thinly sliced
4 tbsp dry sherry
150 ml/ ¹/₄ pint/ ²/₃ cup
   vegetable stock

1 Blend the chickpeas (garbanzo beans), marmite, nuts and breadcrumbs in a food processor for 30 seconds. In a frying pan (skillet) sauté the onion and mushrooms in their own juices for 3–4 minutes. Stir in the chick-pea mixture, corn and garlic. Add the sherry, stock, coriander and seasoning and bind the mixture together. Remove from the heat and allow to cool.

2 Roll the pastry out on to a lightly floured surface to form a 35.5 cm/14 inch x 30 cm/12 inch rectangle. Shape the chickpea (garbanzo bean) mixture into a loaf shape and wrap the pastry around it, sealing the edges. Place seam-side down on a dampened baking tray and score the top in a criss-cross pattern. Mix the egg and milk and brush over the pastry. Cook in a preheated oven, 200°C/ 400°F/Gas Mark 6, for 25–30 minutes. Heat the oil for the sauce in a pan and sauté the leek for 5 minutes. Add the sherry and stock, bring to the boil. Simmer for 5 minutes and serve with the roast.

Kidney Bean Kiev

Serves 4

INGREDIENTS

GARLIC BUTTER:
100 g/3½ oz/ 8 tbsp butter
3 garlic cloves, crushed
1 tbsp chopped parsley

BEAN PATTIES:
650 g/1 lb 7 oz canned red
    kidney beans
150 g/5½ oz/1¼ cups fresh
    white breadcrumbs
25 g/1 oz/2 tbsp butter

1 leek, chopped
1 celery stick, chopped
1 tbsp chopped parsley
1 egg, beaten
salt and pepper
vegetable oil, for shallow frying

1 To make the garlic butter, put the butter, garlic and parsley in a bowl and blend together with a wooden spoon. Place the garlic butter mixture on to a sheet of baking parchment, roll into a cigar shape and wrap in the baking parchment. Leave to chill in the refrigerator.

2 Using a potato masher, mash the red kidney beans in a mixing bowl and stir in 75g /2¾ oz/ ¾ cup of the breadcrumbs until thoroughly blended.

3 Melt the butter in a frying pan (skillet) and sauté the leek and celery for 3–4 minutes, stirring.

4 Add the bean mixture to the pan together with the parsley, season with salt and pepper to taste and mix well. Remove from the heat and leave to cool slightly.

5 Shape the bean mixture into 4 equal sized ovals.

6 Slice the garlic butter into 4 and place a slice in the centre of each bean patty. Mould the bean mixture around the garlic butter to encase it completely.

7 Dip each bean patty into the beaten egg to coat and then roll in the remaining breadcrumbs.

8 Heat a little oil in a frying pan (skillet) and fry the patties, turning once, for 7–10 minutes or until golden. Serve.

Cashew Nut Paella

Serves 4

INGREDIENTS

2 tbsp olive oil
1 tbsp butter
1 red onion, chopped
150 g/5½ oz/1 cup arborio rice
1 tsp ground turmeric
1 tsp ground cumin
½ tsp chilli powder
3 garlic cloves, crushed

1 green chilli, sliced
1 green (bell) pepper, diced
1 red (bell) pepper, diced
75 g/2¾ oz baby corn cobs,
   halved lengthwise
2 tbsp pitted black olives
1 large tomato, seeded and diced
450 ml/¾ pint/2 cups

vegetable stock
75 g/2¾ oz/¾ cup unsalted
   cashew nuts
25 g/1 oz/¼ cup frozen peas
2 tbsp chopped parsley
pinch of cayenne pepper
salt and pepper
fresh herbs, to garnish

1 Heat the olive oil and butter in a large frying pan (skillet) or paella pan until the butter has melted.

2 Add the chopped onion to the pan and sauté for 2–3 minutes, stirring, until the onion has softened.

3 Stir in the rice, turmeric, cumin, chilli powder, garlic, chilli, (bell) peppers, corn cobs, olives and tomato and cook over a medium heat for 1–2 minutes, stirring occasionally.

4 Pour in the stock and bring the mixture to the boil. Reduce the heat and cook for 20 minutes, stirring.

5 Add the cashew nuts and peas to the mixture in the pan and cook for a further 5 minutes, stirring occasionally. Season to taste and sprinkle with parsley and cayenne pepper. Transfer to warm serving plates, garnish and serve immediately.

COOK'S TIP

For authenticity and flavour, use a few saffron strands soaked in a little boiling water instead of the turmeric. Saffron has a lovely, nutty flavour.

Vegetable & Tofu (Bean Curd) Strudels

Serves 4

INGREDIENTS

FILLING:

2 tbsp vegetable oil

2 tbsp butter or vegetarian
    margarine

150 g/5½ oz/⅓ cup potatoes
    finely diced

1 leek, shredded

2 garlic cloves, crushed

1 tsp garam masala

½ tsp chilli powder

½ tsp turmeric

50 g/1¾ oz okra, sliced

100 g/3½ oz/1¼ cups button
    mushrooms, sliced

2 tomatoes, diced

225 g/8 oz firm tofu
    (bean curd), diced

12 sheets filo pastry

2 tbsp butter or vegetarian
    margarine, melted

salt and pepper

1 To make the filling, heat the oil and butter in a frying pan (skillet). Add the potatoes and leek and cook for 2–3 minutes, stirring.

2 Add the garlic and spices, okra, mushrooms, tomatoes, tofu (bean curd) and seasoning and cook, stirring, for 5–7 minutes or until tender.

3 Lay the pastry out on a chopping board and brush each individual sheet with butter. Place 3 sheets on top of one another; repeat to make 4 stacks.

4 Spoon a quarter of the filling along the centre of each stack and brush the edges with butter. Fold the short edges in and roll up lengthwise to form a cigar shape; brush the outside with butter. Place the strudels on a greased baking tray (cookie sheet).

5 Cook in a preheated oven, 190°C/375°F/Gas Mark 5, and cook the strudels for 20 minutes or until golden brown. Serve immediately.

COOK'S TIP

Decorate the outside of the strudels with crumpled pastry trimmings before cooking for a really impressive effect.

Vegetable Lasagne

Serves 4

INGREDIENTS

1 aubergine (eggplant), sliced	½ tsp ground cumin	CHEESE SAUCE:
3 tbsp olive oil	2 tomatoes, chopped	2 tbsp butter or vegetarian
2 garlic cloves, crushed	300 ml/½ pint/1¼ cups	margarine
1 red onion, halved and sliced	passata (sieved tomatoes)	1 tbsp flour
1 green (bell) pepper, diced	2 tbsp chopped basil	150 ml/ ¼ pint/ ⅔ cup
1 red (bell) pepper, diced	8 no pre-cook lasagne verdi sheets	vegetable stock
1 yellow (bell) pepper, diced	salt and pepper	300 ml/½ pint/1¼ cups milk
225 g/8 oz /3cups mixed		75 g/2¾ oz/¾ cup vegetarian
mushrooms, sliced		Cheddar, grated
2 celery sticks, sliced		1 tsp Dijon mustard
1 courgette (zucchini), diced		1 tbsp chopped basil
½ tsp chilli powder		1 egg, beaten

1 Place the aubergine (eggplant) slices in a colander, sprinkle with salt and leave for 20 minutes. Rinse under cold water, drain and reserve. Heat the oil in a pan and sauté the garlic and onion for 1–2 minutes. Add the (bell) peppers, mushrooms, celery and courgette (zucchini) and cook for 3–4 minutes, stirring. Stir in the spices and cook for 1 minute. Mix the tomatoes, passata (sieved tomatoes) and basil together and season well.

2 For the sauce, melt the butter in a pan, add the flour and cook for 1 minute. Remove from the heat and stir in the stock and milk. Return to the heat and add half of the cheese and the mustard. Boil, stirring, until thickened. Stir in the basil and season. Remove from the heat and stir in the egg. Place half of the lasagne sheets in an ovenproof dish. Top with half of the vegetables, then half of the tomato sauce. Cover with half the aubergines (eggplants). Repeat and spoon the cheese sauce on top. Sprinkle with cheese and cook in a preheated oven, 180°C/350°F/Gas 4, for 40 minutes.

Lentil & Rice Casserole

Serves 4

INGREDIENTS

225 g/8 oz/1¼ cups red
    split lentils
50 g/1¾ oz/⅓ cup long-grain
    white rice
1 litre/1¾ pints/5 cups vegetable
    stock
150 ml/¼ pint/⅔ cup dry
    white wine
1 leek, cut into chunks

3 garlic cloves, crushed
400 g/14 oz can
    chopped tomatoes
1 tsp ground cumin
1 tsp chilli powder
1 tsp garam masala
1 red (bell) pepper, sliced
100 g/3½ oz small
    broccoli florets

8 baby corn cobs,
    halved lengthwise
50 g/1¾ oz French (green)
    beans, halved
1 tbsp fresh basil, shredded
salt and pepper
fresh basil sprigs, to garnish

1 Place the lentils, rice, vegetable stock and white wine in a flameproof casserole dish and cook over a gentle heat for 20 minutes, stirring occasionally.

2 Add the leek, garlic, tomatoes, cumin, chilli powder, garam masala, (bell) pepper, broccoli, corn cobs and French (green) beans.

3 Bring the mixture to the boil, reduce the heat, cover and simmer for a further 10–15 minutes or until the vegetables are tender.

4 Add the shredded basil and season with salt and pepper to taste.

5 Garnish with fresh basil sprigs and serve immediately.

VARIATION

You can vary the rice in this recipe – use brown or wild rice, if you prefer.

Vegetable Hot Pot

Serves 4

INGREDIENTS

2 large potatoes, thinly sliced
2 tbsp vegetable oil
1 red onion, halved and sliced
1 leek, sliced
2 garlic cloves, crushed
1 carrot, cut into chunks
100 g/3½ oz broccoli florets

100 g/3½ oz cauliflower florets
2 small turnips, quartered
1 tbsp plain (all-purpose) flour
700 ml/1 ¼ pints/3½ cups
    vegetable stock
150 ml/¼ pint/⅔ cup dry cider
1 dessert (eating) apple, sliced

2 tbsp chopped sage
pinch of cayenne pepper
50 g/1¾ oz/½ cup vegetarian
    Cheddar cheese, grated
salt and pepper

1 Cook the potato slices in a saucepan of boiling water for 10 minutes. Drain thoroughly and reserve.

2 Heat the oil in a flameproof casserole dish and sauté the onion, leek and garlic for 2–3 minutes. Add the remaining vegetables and cook for a further 3–4 minutes, stirring.

3 Stir in the flour and cook for 1 minute. Gradually add the stock and cider and bring the mixture to the boil. Add the apple, sage and cayenne pepper and season well. Remove the dish from the heat. Transfer the vegetables to an ovenproof dish.

4 Arrange the potato slices on top of the vegetable mixture to cover.

5 Sprinkle the cheese on top of the potato slices and cook in a preheated oven, 190°C/375°F/Gas Mark 5, for 30–35 minutes or until the potato is golden brown and beginning to crispen slightly around the edges. Serve immediately.

COOK'S TIP

If the potato begins to brown too quickly, cover with foil for the last 10 minutes of cooking time to prevent the top from burning.

Vegetable Chop Suey

Serves 4

INGREDIENTS

2 tbsp peanut oil
1 onion, chopped
3 garlic cloves, chopped
1 green (bell) pepper, diced
1 red (bell) pepper, diced
75 g/2¾ oz broccoli florets

1 courgette (zucchini), sliced
25 g/1 oz French (green) beans
1 carrot, cut into matchsticks
100 g/3½ oz bean sprouts
2 tsp light brown sugar
2 tbsp light soy sauce

125 ml/4 fl oz/½ cup
vegetable stock
salt and pepper
noodles, to serve

1 Heat the oil in a preheated wok until almost smoking. Add the onion and garlic and stir-fry for 30 seconds.

2 Stir in the (bell) peppers, broccoli, courgette (zucchini), beans and carrot and stir-fry for a further 2–3 minutes.

3 Add the bean sprouts, light brown sugar, soy sauce and vegetable stock. Season with salt and pepper to taste and cook for about 2 minutes.

4 Transfer the vegetables to serving plates and serve immediately with noodles.

COOK'S TIP

The clever design of a wok, with its spherical base and high sloping sides, enables the food to be tossed so that it is cooked quickly and evenly. It is essential to heat the wok sufficiently before you add the ingredients to ensure quick and even cooking.

COOK'S TIP

Ensure that the vegetable pieces are of the same size in order that they all cook in the stated time.

VARIATION

Add 1 tbsp chilli oil for a hotter flavour and add cashew nuts for extra crunch.

Vegetable Toad-in-the-hole

Serves 4

INGREDIENTS

BATTER:

100 g/3½ oz/¾ cup plain (all-purpose) flour

2 eggs, beaten

200 ml/7 fl oz/¾ cup milk

2 tbsp wholegrain mustard

2 tbsp vegetable oil

FILLING:

2 tbsp butter

2 garlic cloves, crushed

1 onion, cut into eight

75 g/2¾ oz baby carrots, halved lengthwise

50 g/1¾ oz French (green) beans

50 g/1¾ oz canned sweetcorn, drained

2 tomatoes, seeded and cut into chunks

1 tsp wholegrain mustard

1 tbsp chopped mixed herbs

salt and pepper

1 To make the batter, sieve the flour and a pinch of salt into a large bowl. Make a well in the centre and beat in the eggs and milk to make a batter. Stir in the mustard and leave to stand.

2 Pour the oil into a shallow ovenproof dish and heat in a preheated oven, 200°C/400°F/ Gas Mark 6, for 10 minutes.

3 To make the filling, melt the butter in a frying pan (skillet) and sauté the garlic and onion for 2 minutes, stirring. Cook the carrots and beans in a saucepan of boiling water for 7 minutes or until tender. Drain well.

4 Add the sweetcorn and tomato to the frying pan (skillet) with the mustard and herbs. Season well and add the carrots and beans.

5 Remove the dish from the oven and pour in the batter. Spoon the vegetables into the centre, return to the oven and cook for 30–35 minutes until the batter has risen and set. Serve the vegetable toad-in-the-hole immediately.

COOK'S TIP

It is important that the oil is hot before adding the batter so that the batter begins to cook and rise immediately.

Vegetable Jalousie

Serves 4

INGREDIENTS

450 g/1 lb prepared puff pastry
1 egg, beaten

FILLING:
2 tbsp butter or vegetarian
    margarine
1 leek, shredded

2 garlic cloves, crushed
1 red (bell) pepper, sliced
1 yellow (bell) pepper, sliced
50 g/1³⁄₄ oz mushrooms, sliced
75 g/2³⁄₄ oz small
    asparagus spears
2 tbsp flour

85 ml/3 fl oz/6 tbsp
    vegetable stock
85 ml/3 fl oz/6 tbsp milk
4 tbsp dry white wine
1 tbsp chopped oregano
salt and pepper

1 Melt the butter or margarine in a pan and sauté the leek and garlic for 2 minutes, stirring. Add the remaining vegetables and cook, stirring, for 3–4 minutes.

2 Add the flour and cook for 1 minute. Remove the pan from the heat and stir in the vegetable stock, milk and white wine. Return the pan to the heat and bring to the boil, stirring, until thickened. Stir in the oregano and season with salt and pepper to taste.

3 Roll half of the pastry out on a lightly floured surface to form a rectangle 42.5 cm/15 inches x 15 cm/6 inches.

4 Roll out the other half of the pastry to the same shape, but a little larger. Put the smaller rectangle on a baking tray (cookie sheet) lined with dampened baking parchment.

5 Spoon the filling on top of the smaller rectangle, leaving a 1.25 cm/¹⁄₂ inch clean edge.

6 Cut parallel slits across the larger rectangle to within 2.5 cm/1 inch of each edge.

7 Brush the edge of the smaller rectangle with egg and place the larger rectangle on top, sealing the edges well.

8 Brush the whole jalousie with egg and cook in a preheated oven, 200°C/400°F/Gas Mark 6, for 30–35 minutes until risen and golden. Serve immediately.

Cauliflower, Broccoli & Cheese Flan

Serves 8

INGREDIENTS

PASTRY:

175 g/6 oz/11/4 cups plain (all-purpose) flour

pinch of salt

1/2 tsp paprika

1 tsp dried thyme

75 g/2³/4 oz/6 tbsp vegetarian margarine

3 tbsp water

FILLING:

100 g/3¹/2 oz cauliflower florets

100 g/3¹/2 oz broccoli florets

1 onion, cut into eight

2 tbsp butter or vegetarian margarine

1 tbsp plain (all-purpose) flour

85 ml/3 fl oz/6 tbsp vegetable stock

125 ml/4 fl oz/8 tbsp milk

75 g/2³/4 oz/³/4 cup vegetarian Cheddar cheese, grated

salt and pepper

paprika and thyme, to garnish

1 To make the pastry, sieve the flour and salt into a bowl. Add the paprika and thyme and rub in the margarine. Stir in the water and bind to form a dough.

2 Roll the pastry out on a floured surface and use to line an 18cm/7 inch loose-bottomed flan tin (pan). Prick the base with a fork and line with baking parchment. Fill with ceramic baking beans and bake in a preheated oven, at 190°C/375°F/ Gas Mark 5, for 15 minutes. Remove the parchment and beans and return the pastry case to the oven for 5 minutes.

3 To make the filling, cook the vegetables in a pan of boiling water for 10–12 minutes until tender. Drain and reserve.

4 Melt the butter in a pan. Add the flour and cook, stirring, for 1 minute.

Remove from the heat, stir in the stock and milk and return to the heat. Bring to the boil, stirring, and add 50 g/ 1¹/4 oz/¹/2 cup of the cheese. Season.

5 Spoon the cauliflower, broccoli and onion into the pastry case. Pour over the sauce and sprinkle with the cheese. Return to the oven for 10 minutes until the cheese is bubbling. Dust with paprika, garnish and serve.

Roast (Bell) Pepper Tart

Serves 8

INGREDIENTS

PASTRY:

175 g/6 oz/1¼ cups plain
(all-purpose) flour

pinch of salt

75 g/2¾ oz/6 tbsp butter or
vegetarian margarine

2 tbsp green pitted olives, finely
chopped

3 tbsp cold water

FILLING:

1 red (bell) pepper

1 green (bell) pepper

1 yellow (bell) pepper

2 garlic cloves, crushed

2 tbsp olive oil

100 g/3½ oz/1 cup Mozzarella
cheese, grated

2 eggs

150 ml/5 fl oz/⅔ cup milk

1 tbsp chopped basil

salt and pepper

1 To make the pastry, sieve the flour and a pinch of salt into a bowl. Rub in the butter or margarine until the mixture resembles breadcrumbs. Add the olives and cold water, bringing the mixture together to form a dough.

2 Roll the dough out on to a floured surface and use to line a 20 cm/8 inch loose-bottomed flan tin (pan). Prick the base with a fork and leave to chill.

3 Cut the (bell) peppers in half lengthwise and lay skin-side uppermost on a baking tray (cookie sheet). Mix the garlic and oil and brush over the (bell) peppers. Cook in a preheated oven, 200°C/400°F/Gas Mark 6, for 20 minutes or until beginning to char slightly. Let the (bell) peppers cool slightly and thinly slice. Arrange in the base of the pastry case, layering with the Mozzarella cheese.

4 Beat the egg and milk and add the basil. Season and pour over the (bell) peppers. Put the tart on a baking tray (cookie sheet) and return to the oven for 20 minutes or until set. Serve hot or cold.

Vegetable Biryani

Serves 4

INGREDIENTS

1 large potato, cubed
100 g/3¹/₂ oz baby carrots
50 g/1³/₄ oz okra, thickly sliced
2 celery sticks, sliced
75 g/2³/₄ oz baby button
    mushrooms, halved
1 aubergine (eggplant), halved
    and sliced

300 ml/¹/₂ pint/1¹/₄ cups natural
    (unsweetened) yogurt
1 tbsp grated root ginger
2 large onions, grated
4 garlic cloves, crushed
1 tsp turmeric
1 tbsp curry powder
2 tbsp butter

2 onions, sliced
225 g/8 oz/1 ¹/₄ cups
    basmati rice
chopped coriander (cilantro),
    to garnish

1 Cook the potato cubes, carrots and okra in a pan of boiling salted water for 7–8 minutes. Drain well and place in a large bowl. Mix with the celery, mushrooms and aubergine (eggplant).

2 Mix the natural (unsweetened) yogurt, ginger, grated onions, garlic, turmeric and curry powder and spoon over the vegetables, tossing to coat thoroughly. Leave to marinate for at least 2 hours.

3 Heat the butter in a frying pan (skillet) and cook the sliced onions for 5–6 minutes until golden brown. Remove a few onions from the pan and reserve for garnishing.

4 Cook the rice in a pan of boiling water for 7 minutes. Drain well.

5 Add the marinated vegetables to the onions and cook for 10 minutes.

6 Put half of the rice in a 2 litre/3¹/₂ pint casserole dish. Spoon the vegetables on top and cover with the remaining rice. Cover and cook in a preheated oven, 190°C/375°F/Gas Mark 5, for 20–25 minutes or until the rice is tender.

7 Spoon the biryani on to a serving plate, garnish with the reserved onions and chopped coriander (cilantro) and serve immediately.

Baked Cheese & Tomato Macaroni

Serves 4

INGREDIENTS

225 g/8 oz/2 cups elbow
  macaroni
175 g/6 oz/1½ cups grated
  vegetarian cheese
100 g/3½ oz/1 cup grated
  Parmesan cheese
4 tbsp fresh white breadcrumbs

1 tbsp chopped basil
1 tbsp butter or margarine

TOMATO SAUCE:
1 tbsp olive oil
1 shallot, finely chopped
2 garlic cloves, crushed

450 g/1 lb canned chopped
  tomatoes
1 tbsp chopped basil
salt and pepper

1 To make the tomato sauce, heat the oil in a saucepan and sauté the shallots and garlic for 1 minute. Add the tomatoes, basil, salt and pepper to taste and cook over a medium heat, stirring, for 10 minutes.

2 Meanwhile, cook the macaroni in a pan of boiling salted water for 8 minutes or until just undercooked. Drain.

3 Mix both of the cheeses together.

4 Grease a deep, ovenproof dish. Spoon a third of the tomato sauce into the base of the dish, top with a third of the macaroni and then a third of the cheeses. Season with salt and pepper. Repeat the layers twice.

5 Combine the breadcrumbs and basil and sprinkle over the top. Dot with the butter or margarine and cook in a preheated oven, 190°C/375°F/Gas Mark 5, for 25 minutes or until the dish is golden brown and bubbling. Serve.

COOK'S TIP

Use other pasta shapes, such as penne, if you have them to hand, instead of the macaroni.

Chickpea (Garbanzo Bean) & Vegetable Casserole

Serves 4

INGREDIENTS

1 tbsp olive oil	450 ml/¾ pint/3¾ cups vegetable stock	1 tsp ground coriander
1 red onion, halved and sliced		½ tsp paprika
3 garlic cloves, crushed	85 ml/3 fl oz/6 tbsp dry white wine	salt and pepper
225 g/8 oz spinach		fennel fronds, to garnish
1 fennel bulb, cut into eight	400 g/14 oz can chickpeas (garbanzo beans), drained	
1 red (bell) pepper, cubed	1 bay leaf	
1 tbsp plain (all-purpose) flour		

1 Heat the olive oil in a large flameproof casserole dish and sauté the onion and garlic for 1 minute, stirring. Add the spinach and cook for 4 minutes or until wilted.

2 Add the fennel and (bell) pepper and cook for 2 minutes, stirring.

3 Stir in the flour and cook for 1 minute.

4 Add the stock, wine, chickpeas (garbanzo beans), bay leaf, coriander and paprika, cover and cook for 30 minutes. Season to taste, garnish with fennel fronds and serve immediately.

VARIATION

Replace the coriander with nutmeg, if you prefer, as it works particularly well with spinach.

COOK'S TIP

Use other canned pulses or mixed beans instead of the chickpeas (garbanzo beans), if you prefer.

Sweet & Sour Vegetables & Tofu (Bean Curd)

Serves 4

INGREDIENTS

1 tbsp peanut oil
2 garlic cloves, crushed
1 tsp grated root ginger
50 g/1¾ oz baby corn cobs
50 g/1¾ oz mangetout
    (snow peas)
1 carrot, cut into matchsticks
1 green (bell) pepper, cut

into matchsticks
8 spring onions (scallions),
    trimmed
50 g/1¾ oz canned bamboo
    shoots
225 g/8 oz marinated firm tofu
    (bean curd), cubed
2 tbsp dry sherry

2 tbsp rice vinegar
2 tbsp clear honey
1 tbsp light soy sauce
150 ml/¼ pint/⅔ cup
    vegetable stock
1 tbsp cornflour (cornstarch)

1 Heat the oil in a preheated wok until almost smoking.

2 Add the garlic and grated root ginger and cook for 30 seconds, stirring frequently.

3 Add the baby corn cobs, mangetout (snow peas), carrot and (bell) pepper and stir-fry for about 5 minutes or until the vegetables are tender.

4 Add the spring onions (scallions), bamboo shoots and tofu (bean curd) and cook for a further 2 minutes.

5 Stir in the sherry, rice vinegar, honey, soy sauce, vegetable stock and cornflour (cornstarch) and bring to the boil. Reduce the heat and simmer for 2 minutes. Transfer to serving dishes and serve immediately.

VARIATION

You can replace any of the vegetables in this dish with others of your choice. For a colourful, attractive stir-fry, select vegetables with bright, contrasting colours.

Spicy Potato & Lemon Casserole

Serves 4

INGREDIENTS

100 ml/3¹/₂ fl oz/¹/₂ cup
    olive oil
2 red onions, cut into eight
3 garlic cloves, crushed
2 tsp ground cumin
2 tsp ground coriander

pinch of cayenne pepper
1 carrot, thickly sliced
2 small turnips, quartered
1 courgette (zucchini), sliced
450 g/1 lb potatoes, thickly sliced
juice and rind of 2 large lemons

300 ml/¹/₂ pint/1 ¹/₄ cups
    vegetable stock
2 tbsp chopped
    coriander (cilantro)
salt and pepper

1 Heat the olive oil in a flameproof casserole.

2 Add the red onion and sauté for 3 minutes, stirring.

3 Add the garlic and cook for 30 seconds. Mix in the spices and cook for 1 minute, stirring.

4 Add the carrot, turnips, courgette (zucchini) and potatoes and stir to coat in the oil.

5 Add the lemon juice and rind, stock and salt and pepper to taste, cover and cook over a medium heat for 20–30 minutes, stirring occasionally.

6 Remove the lid, sprinkle in the coriander (cilantro) and stir well. Serve immediately.

COOK'S TIP

Check the vegetables whilst cooking as they may begin to stick to the pan. Add a little more boiling water or stock if necessary.

COOK'S TIP

A selection of spices and herbs is important for adding variety to your cooking – add to your range each time you try a new recipe.

Vegetable Cannelloni

Serves 4

INGREDIENTS

1 aubergine (eggplant)	12 cannelloni tubes	2 x 400 g/14 oz cans
125 ml/^{1}/4 fl oz/^{1}/2 cup olive oil	salt and pepper	chopped tomatoes
225 g/8 oz spinach		1 tsp caster (superfine) sugar
2 garlic cloves, crushed	TOMATO SAUCE:	2 tbsp chopped basil
1 tsp ground cumin	1 tbsp olive oil	50 g/1^3/4 oz/^{1}/2 cup
75 g/2^3/4 oz/1 cup	1 onion, chopped	Mozzarella, sliced
mushrooms, chopped	2 garlic cloves, crushed	

1 Cut the aubergine (eggplant) into small dice.

2 Heat the oil in a frying pan (skillet) and cook the aubergine (eggplant) for 2–3 minutes.

3 Add the spinach, garlic, cumin and mushrooms. Season and cook for 2–3 minutes, stirring. Spoon the mixture into the cannelloni tubes and place in an ovenproof dish in a single layer.

4 To make the sauce, heat the olive oil in a saucepan and sauté the onion and garlic for 1 minute. Add the tomatoes, caster (superfine) sugar and chopped basil and bring to the boil. Reduce the heat and simmer for about 5 minutes. Pour the sauce over the cannelloni tubes.

5 Arrange the sliced Mozzarella on top of the sauce and cook in a preheated oven, 190°C/ 375°F/ Gas Mark 5, for 30 minutes or until the cheese is bubbling and golden brown. Serve immediately.

COOK'S TIP

You can prepare the tomato sauce in advance and store it in the refrigerator for up to 24 hours.

Cauliflower Bake

Serves 4

INGREDIENTS

450 g/1 lb cauliflower, broken into florets
2 large potatoes, cubed
100 g/3½ oz cherry tomatoes

SAUCE:
25 g/1 oz/2 tbsp butter or vegetarian margarine
1 leek, sliced
1 garlic clove, crushed
25 g/1 oz/3 tbsp plain (all-purpose) flour
300 ml/½ pint/1¼ cups milk

75 g/2¾ oz/¾ cup mixed grated cheese, such as vegetarian Cheddar, Parmesan and Gruyère
½ tsp paprika
2 tbsp chopped flat-leaf parsley
salt and pepper
chopped fresh parsley, to garnish

1 Cook the cauliflower in a saucepan of boiling water for 10 minutes. Drain well and reserve. Meanwhile, cook the potatoes in a pan of boiling water for 10 minutes, drain and reserve.

2 To make the sauce, melt the butter or margarine in a saucepan and sauté the leek and garlic for 1 minute. Add the flour and cook for 1 minute. Remove the pan from the heat and gradually stir in the milk, 50 g/1¾ oz/½ cup of the cheese, the paprika and parsley. Return the pan to the heat and bring to the boil, stirring. Season with salt and pepper to taste.

3 Spoon the cauliflower into a deep ovenproof dish. Add the cherry tomatoes and top with the potatoes. Pour the sauce over the potatoes and sprinkle on the remaining cheese.

4 Cook in a preheated oven, 180°C/350°F/Gas Mark 4, for 20 minutes or until the vegetables are cooked through and the cheese is golden brown and bubbling. Garnish and serve immediately.

VARIATION

This dish could be made with broccoli instead of the cauliflower as an alternative.

Leek & Herb Soufflé

Serves 4

INGREDIENTS

350 g/12 oz baby leeks	2 eggs, separated
1 tbsp olive oil	2 tbsp chopped mixed herbs
125 ml/4 fl oz/½ cup	2 tbsp natural
vegetable stock	(unsweetened) yogurt
50 g/1¾ oz/½ cup walnuts	salt and pepper

1 Using a sharp knife, chop the leeks finely.

2 Heat the oil in a frying pan (skillet) and sauté the leeks for 2–3 minutes.

3 Add the stock to the pan and cook over a gentle heat for a further 5 minutes.

4 Place the walnuts in a food processor and blend until finely chopped.

5 Add the leek mixture to the nuts and blend to form a purée. Transfer to a mixing bowl.

6 Combine the egg yolks, herbs and yogurt and pour into the leek purée. Season with salt and pepper to taste and mix well.

7 In a separate mixing bowl, whisk the egg whites until firm peaks form.

8 Fold the egg whites into the leek mixture. Spoon the mixture into a lightly greased 900 ml/1½ pint ramekin dish and place on a warmed baking tray (cookie sheet).

9 Cook in a preheated oven, 180°C/350°F/ Gas Mark 4, for 35–40 minutes or until set. Serve the soufflé immediately.

Artichoke & Cheese Tart

Serves 8

INGREDIENTS

175 g/6 oz/1 ¼ cups wholemeal
   (whole wheat) flour
2 garlic cloves, crushed
75 g/2¾ oz/6 tbsp butter or
   vegetarian margarine
salt and pepper

FILLING:
2 tbsp olive oil
1 red onion, halved and sliced
10 canned or fresh
   artichoke hearts
100 g/3½ oz/1 cup vegetarian

Cheddar, grated
50 g/1¾ oz/½ cup Gorgonzola
   cheese, crumbled
2 eggs, beaten
1 tbsp chopped fresh rosemary
150 ml/¼ pint/⅔ cup milk

1 To make the pastry, sieve the flour into a mixing bowl, add a pinch of salt and the garlic. Rub in the butter until the mixture resembles breadcrumbs. Stir in 3 tablespoons of water and bring the mixture together to form a dough.

2 Roll the pastry out on a lightly floured surface to fit a 20cm/8 inch flan tin (pan). Prick the pastry with a fork.

3 Heat the oil in a frying pan (skillet) and sauté the onion for 3 minutes. Add the artichoke hearts and cook for a further 2 minutes.

4 Mix the cheeses with the beaten eggs, rosemary and milk. Stir in the drained artichoke mixture and season to taste.

5 Spoon the artichoke and cheese mixture into the pastry case and cook in a preheated oven, 200°C/400°F/Gas Mark 6,

for 25 minutes or until cooked and set. Serve the flan hot or cold.

COOK'S TIP

Gently press the centre of the flan with your fingertip to test if it is cooked through. It should feel fairly firm, but not solid. If overcooked the flan will begin to 'weep'.

Tagliatelle with Courgette (Zucchini) Sauce

Serves 4

INGREDIENTS

650 g/1 lb 7 oz courgettes (zucchini)	juice of 1 large lemon
6 tbsp olive oil	5 tbsp single (light) cream
3 garlic cloves, crushed	4 tbsp grated Parmesan cheese
3 tbsp chopped basil	225 g/8 oz tagliatelle
2 red chillies, sliced	salt and pepper

1 Using a vegetable peeler, slice the courgettes (zucchini) into thin ribbons.

2 Heat the oil in a frying pan (skillet) and sauté the garlic for 30 seconds.

3 Add the courgettes (zucchini) and cook over a gentle heat, stirring, for 5–7 minutes.

4 Stir in the basil, chillies, lemon juice, single (light) cream and grated Parmesan cheese and season with salt and pepper to taste.

5 Meanwhile, cook the tagliatelle in a large pan of lightly salted boiling water for 10 minutes until 'al dente'. Drain the pasta thoroughly and put in a warm serving bowl.

6 Pile the courgette (zucchini) mixture on top of the pasta. Serve immediately.

VARIATION

Lime juice and zest could be used instead of the lemon as an alternative.

Olive, (Bell) Pepper & Cherry Tomato Pasta

Serves 4

INGREDIENTS

225 g/8 oz/2 cups penne
2 tbsp olive oil
2 tbsp butter
2 garlic cloves, crushed
1 green (bell) pepper,
    thinly sliced

1 yellow (bell) pepper,
    thinly sliced
16 cherry tomatoes, halved
1 tbsp chopped oregano
125 ml/4 fl oz/½ cup dry
    white wine

2 tbsp quartered, pitted
    black olives
75 g/2¾ oz rocket (arugula)
salt and pepper
fresh oregano sprigs, to garnish

1 Cook the pasta in a saucepan of boiling salted water for 8–10 minutes or until 'al dente'. Drain thoroughly.

2 Heat the oil and butter in a pan until the butter melts. Sauté the garlic for 30 seconds. Add the (bell) peppers and cook for 3–4 minutes, stirring.

3 Stir in the cherry tomatoes, oregano, wine and olives and cook for 3–4 minutes. Season well with salt and pepper and stir in the rocket until just wilted.

4 Transfer the pasta to a serving dish, spoon over the sauce and mix well. Garnish and serve.

COOK'S TIP

Ensure that the saucepan is large enough to prevent the pasta from sticking together during cooking.

Spinach & Pine Kernel (Nut) Pasta

Serves 4

INGREDIENTS

225 g/8 oz pasta shapes
    or spaghetti
125 ml/4 fl oz/½ cup olive oil
2 garlic cloves, crushed
1 onion, quartered
    and sliced

3 large flat mushrooms, sliced
225 g/8 oz spinach
2 tbsp pine kernels (nuts)
85 ml/3 fl oz/6 tbsp dry
    white wine
salt and pepper

Parmesan shavings,
    to garnish

1 Cook the pasta in a saucepan of boiling salted water for 8–10 minutes or until 'al dente'. Drain well.

2 Meanwhile, heat the oil in a large saucepan and sauté the garlic and onion for 1 minute.

3 Add the sliced mushrooms and cook for 2 minutes, stirring occasionally.

4 Add the spinach and cook for 4–5 minutes

or until the spinach has wilted.

5 Stir in the pine kernels (nuts) and wine, season well and cook for 1 minute.

6 Transfer the pasta to a warm serving bowl and toss the sauce into it, mixing well. Garnish with shavings of Parmesan cheese and serve.

COOK'S TIP

Freshly grate a little nutmeg over the dish for extra flavour as it is particularly good with spinach.

COOK'S TIP

'Al dente' means that the pasta should be tender but still have a bite to it.

Tofu (Bean Curd) & Vegetable Stir-Fry

Serves 4

INGREDIENTS

175 g/6 oz/1¼ cups
   potatoes, cubed
1 tbsp olive oil
1 red onion, sliced
225 g/8 oz firm tofu
   (bean curd), diced

2 courgettes (zucchini), diced
8 canned artichoke
   hearts, halved
150 ml/¼ pint/⅔ cup passata
   (sieved tomatoes)
1 tsp caster (superfine) sugar

2 tbsp chopped basil
salt and pepper

1 Cook the potatoes in a saucepan of boiling water for 10 minutes. Drain thoroughly and set aside until required.

2 Heat the oil in a large frying pan (skillet) and sauté the red onion for 2 minutes until the onion has softened, stirring.

3 Stir in the tofu (bean curd) and courgettes (zucchini) and cook for 3–4 minutes until they begin to brown slightly. Add the potatoes, stirring to mix.

4 Stir in the artichoke hearts, passata (sieved tomatoes), sugar and basil, season with salt and pepper and cook for a further 5 minutes, stirring well. Transfer the stir-fry to serving dishes and serve immediately.

COOK'S TIP

Canned artichoke hearts should be drained thoroughly and rinsed before use because they often have salt added.

VARIATION

Aubergines (eggplants) could be used instead of the courgettes (zucchini), if preferred.

Cantonese Garden Vegetable Stir-Fry

Serves 4

INGREDIENTS

2 tbsp peanut oil
1 tsp Chinese five-spice powder
75 g/2¾ oz baby carrots, halved
2 celery sticks, sliced
2 baby leeks, sliced
50 g/1¾ oz mangetout
  (snow peas)

4 baby courgettes (zucchini),
  halved lengthwise
8 baby corn cobs
225 g/8 oz firm marinated
  tofu (bean curd), cubed
4 tbsp fresh orange juice
1 tbsp clear honey

celery leaves and orange zest,
  to garnish
cooked rice or noodles, to serve

1 Heat the oil in a preheated wok until almost smoking. Add the Chinese five-spice powder, carrots, celery, leeks, mangetout (snow peas), courgettes (zucchini) and corn cobs and stir-fry for 3–4 minutes.

2 Add the tofu (bean curd) and cook for a further 2 minutes, stirring.

3 Stir in the orange juice and honey, reduce the heat and cook for 1–2 minutes.

4 Transfer the stir-fry to a serving dish, garnish with celery leaves and orange zest and serve with rice or noodles.

COOK'S TIP

Chinese five-spice powder is a mixture of fennel, star anise, cinnamon bark, cloves and Szechuan pepper. It is very pungent so should be used sparingly. If kept in an airtight container, it will keep indefinitely.

Risotto Verde

Serves 4

INGREDIENTS

1.75 litres/3 pints/7½ cups
vegetable stock
2 tbsp olive oil
2 garlic cloves, crushed
2 leeks, shredded

225 g/8 oz/1¼ cups arborio rice
300 ml/½ pint/1¼ cups dry
white wine
4 tbsp chopped mixed herbs
225 g/8 oz baby spinach

3 tbsp natural (unsweetened)
yogurt
salt and pepper
shredded leek, to garnish

1 Pour the stock into a large saucepan and bring to the boil. Reduce the heat to a simmer.

2 Meanwhile, heat the oil in a separate pan and sauté the garlic and leeks for 2–3 minutes until softened.

3 Stir in the rice and cook for 2 minutes, stirring until well coated.

4 Pour in half of the wine and a little of the hot stock. Cook over a gentle heat until all of the liquid has been absorbed. Add the remaining stock and wine and cook over a low heat for 25 minutes or until the rice is creamy.

5 Stir in the chopped mixed herbs and baby spinach, season well with salt and pepper and cook for 2 minutes.

6 Stir in the natural (unsweetened) yogurt, garnish with the shredded leek and serve immediately.

COOK'S TIP

Do not hurry the process of cooking the risotto as the rice must absorb the liquid slowly in order for it to reach the correct consistency.

Baked Pasta in Tomato Sauce

Serves 8

INGREDIENTS

100 g/3½ oz/1 cup pasta shapes,
    such as penne or casareccia
1 tbsp olive oil
1 leek, chopped
3 garlic cloves, crushed
1 green (bell) pepper, chopped
400 g/14 oz can
    chopped tomatoes
2 tbsp chopped, pitted

black olives
2 eggs, beaten
1 tbsp chopped basil

TOMATO SAUCE:
1 tbsp olive oil
1 onion, chopped
225 g/8 oz can

chopped tomatoes
1 tsp caster (superfine) sugar
2 tbsp tomato purée (paste)
150 ml/¼ pint/⅔ cup
    vegetable stock
salt and pepper

1 Cook the pasta in a saucepan of boiling salted water for 8 minutes. Drain thoroughly.

2 Meanwhile, heat the oil in a saucepan and sauté the leek and garlic for 2 minutes, stirring. Add the (bell) pepper, tomatoes and olives and cook for a further 5 minutes.

3 Remove the pan from the heat and stir in the pasta, beaten eggs and basil. Season well, and spoon into a lightly greased 1 litre/2 pint ovenproof pudding basin.

4 Place the pudding basin in a roasting tin (pan) and half-fill the tin (pan) with boiling water. Cover and cook in a preheated oven, 180°C/350°F/Gas Mark 6, for 40 minutes until set.

5 To make the sauce, heat the oil in a pan and sauté the onion for 2 minutes. Add the remaining ingredients and cook for 10 minutes. Put the sauce in a food processor or blender and blend until smooth. Return to a clean saucepan and heat until hot.

6 Turn the pasta out of the pudding basin on to a warm plate. Slice and serve with the tomato sauce.

Spaghetti with Pear & Walnut Sauce

Serves 4

INGREDIENTS

225 g/8 oz spaghetti
2 small ripe pears, peeled
    and sliced
150 ml/¼ pint/²/₃ cup
    vegetable stock
85 ml/3 fl oz/6 tbsp dry
    white wine

2 tbsp butter
1 tbsp olive oil
1 red onion, quartered and sliced
1 garlic clove, crushed
50 g/1¾ oz/½ cup
    walnut halves
2 tbsp chopped oregano

1 tbsp lemon juice
75 g/2¾ oz/¾ cup
    dolcelatte cheese
salt and pepper
fresh oregano sprigs, to garnish

1 Cook the pasta in a saucepan of boiling salted water for 8–10 minutes or until 'al dente'. Drain thoroughly and keep warm until required.

2 Meanwhile, place the pears in a pan and pour over the stock and wine. Poach the pears over a gentle heat for 10 minutes. Drain and reserve the cooking liquid and pears.

3 Heat the butter and oil in a saucepan until the butter melts, then sauté the onion and garlic for 2–3 minutes, stirring.

4 Add the walnuts, oregano and lemon juice, stirring.

5 Stir in the reserved pears with 4 tablespoons of the poaching liquid.

6 Crumble the dolcelatte cheese into the pan and cook over a gentle heat, stirring occasionally, for 1–2 minutes or until the cheese just begins to melt. Season the sauce with salt and pepper to taste.

7 Toss the pasta into the sauce, garnish and serve.

COOK'S TIP

You can use any good-flavoured blue cheese for this dish. Other varieties to try are Roquefort, which has a very strong flavour, Gorgonzola or Stilton.

Side Dishes

If you are running short of ideas for interesting side dishes to serve with your main meals, these recipes will be a welcome inspiration. An ideal accompaniment complements the main dish both visually and nutritionally. Many main dishes will be rich in protein, therefore the side dishes in this chapter have been created to be a little lighter in texture but still packed full of colour and flavour. They have been cooked in many different ways – there are bakes, fries, steamed vegetables and braises, all of which are perfect accompaniments for all occasions.

This chapter also contains a selection of delicious salads which are bursting with flavour and colour. Make one of these salads to accompany your main meal, or make larger portions to serve alone. Choose the right salad to serve with your main meal – make sure that the flavours and textures complement rather than clash with one another. The secret of a successful salad relies on one important aspect: the freshness of the ingredients. Try some of of the ideas in this chapter and discover some sensational side dishes to add to your repertoire.

Cheese & Potato Layer Bake

Serves 4

INGREDIENTS

450 g/1 lb potatoes	50 g/1¾ oz/½ cup	150 ml/¼ pint/⅔ cup single
1 leek, sliced	Mozzarella, grated	(light) cream
3 garlic cloves, crushed	25 g/1 oz/¼ cup Parmesan	150 ml/¼ pint/⅔ cup milk
50 g/1¾ oz/½ cup vegetarian	cheese, grated	salt and pepper
Cheddar, grated	2 tbsp chopped parsley	freshly chopped flat-leaf parsley,
		to garnish

1 Cook the potatoes in a saucepan of boiling salted water for 10 minutes. Drain well.

2 Cut the potatoes into thin slices. Arrange a layer of potatoes in the base of an ovenproof dish. Layer with a little of the leek, garlic, cheeses and parsley. Season well.

3 Repeat the layers until all of the ingredients have been used, finishing with a layer of cheese on top.

4 Mix the cream and milk together, season with salt and pepper to taste and pour over the potato layers.

5 Cook in a preheated oven, 160°C/325°F/ Gas Mark 3, for 1–1¼ hours or until the cheese is golden brown and bubbling and the potatoes are cooked through.

6 Garnish with freshly chopped flat-leaf parsley and serve immediately.

COOK'S TIP

There is an Italian Parmesan called Grano Padano which is usually vegetarian. As Parmesan quickly loses its 'bite', it is best to buy it in small quantities and grate only as much as you need. Wrap the rest in foil and store in the refrigerator.

Cauliflower & Broccoli with Herb Sauce

Serves 4

INGREDIENTS

2 baby cauliflowers	SAUCE:	5 tbsp chopped coriander
225 g/8 oz broccoli	8 tbsp olive oil	(cilantro)
salt and pepper	4 tbsp butter or vegetarian	5 tbsp grated Cheddar
	margarine	
	2 tsp grated root ginger	
	juice and rind of 2 lemons	

1 Using a sharp knife, cut the cauliflowers in half and the broccoli into very large florets.

2 Cook the cauliflower and broccoli in a saucepan of boiling salted water for 10 minutes. Drain well, transfer to a shallow ovenproof dish and keep warm until required.

3 To make the sauce, put the oil and butter or vegetarian margarine in a pan and heat gently until the butter melts. Add the grated root ginger, lemon juice, lemon rind and coriander (cilantro) and simmer for 2–3 minutes, stirring occasionally.

4 Season the sauce with salt and pepper to taste, then pour over the vegetables in the dish and sprinkle the cheese on top.

5 Cook under a preheated hot grill (broiler) for 2–3 minutes or until the cheese is bubbling and golden. Leave to cool for 1–2 minutes and then serve.

VARIATION

Lime or orange could be used instead of the lemon for a fruity and refreshing sauce.

Indian Spiced Potatoes & Spinach

Serves 4

INGREDIENTS

3 tbsp vegetable oil	1 tsp ground cumin	450 g/1 lb baby spinach
1 red onion, sliced	150 ml/ $^{1}/_{4}$ pint/ $^{2}/_{3}$ cup	1 red chilli, sliced
2 garlic cloves, crushed	vegetable stock	salt and pepper
$^{1}/_{2}$ tsp chilli powder	300 g/10$^{1}/_{2}$ oz/ $^{2}/_{3}$ cup	
2 tsp ground coriander	potatoes, cubed	

1 Heat the oil in a frying pan (skillet) and sauté the onion and garlic for 2–3 minutes, stirring occasionally.

2 Stir in the chilli powder, ground coriander and cumin and cook for a further 30 seconds.

3 Add the vegetable stock, potato and spinach and bring to the boil. Reduce the heat, cover the frying pan (skillet) and simmer for about 10 minutes or until the potatoes are cooked through.

4 Uncover, season to taste, add the chilli and cook for a further 2–3 minutes. Serve.

COOK'S TIP

Be very careful when handling chillies – never touch your face or eyes as the juices can be very painful and always wash your hands thoroughly after preparing chillies. The seeds are the hottest part of the chilli but have less flavour, so these are usually removed before use.

Steamed Vegetables with Vermouth

Serves 4

INGREDIENTS

1 carrot, cut into batons	4 small onions, halved	4 sprigs tarragon
1 fennel bulb, sliced	8 tbsp vermouth	salt and pepper
100 g/3½ oz courgettes	4 tbsp lime juice	fresh tarragon sprigs, to garnish
(zucchini), sliced	zest of 1 lime	
1 red (bell) pepper, sliced	pinch of paprika	

1 Place all of the vegetables in a large bowl and mix well.

2 Cut 4 large squares of baking parchment and place a quarter of the vegetables in the centre of each. Bring the sides of the paper up and pinch together to make an open parcel.

3 Mix together the vermouth, lime juice, lime zest and paprika and pour a quarter of the mixture into each parcel. Season with salt and pepper and add a tarragon sprig to each. Pinch the tops of the parcels together to seal.

4 Place the parcels in a steamer, cover and cook for 15–20 minutes or until the vegetables are tender. Garnish and serve.

COOKS TIP

Vermouth is a fortified white wine flavoured with various herbs and spices. It its available in both sweet and dry forms.

COOK'S TIP

Seal the parcels well to prevent them opening during cooking and causing the juices to evaporate.

Spicy Peas & Spinach

Serves 4

INGREDIENTS

225 g/8 oz/1 1/4 cups green
    split peas
900 g/2 lb spinach
4 tbsp vegetable oil
1 onion, halved and sliced

1 tsp grated root ginger
1 tsp ground cumin
1/2 tsp chilli powder
1/2 tsp ground coriander
2 garlic cloves, crushed

300 ml/1/2 pint/1 1/4 cups
    vegetable stock
salt and pepper
fresh coriander (cilantro) sprigs
    and lime wedges, to garnish

1 Rinse the peas under cold running water. Transfer to a mixing bowl, cover with cold water and leave to soak for 2 hours. Drain well.

2 Meanwhile, cook the spinach in a large saucepan for 5 minutes until wilted. Drain well and roughly chop.

3 Heat the oil in a large saucepan and sauté the onion, spices and garlic. Sauté for 2–3 minutes, stirring well.

4 Add the peas and spinach and stir in the stock. Cover and simmer for 10–15 minutes or until the peas are cooked and the liquid has been absorbed. Season with salt and pepper to taste, garnish and serve.

COOK'S TIP

Once the peas have been added, stir occasionally to prevent them from sticking to the pan.

VARIATION

If you do not have time to soak the green peas, canned lentils are a good substitute but remember to drain and rinse them first.

Beans in Lemon & Herb Sauce

Serves 4

INGREDIENTS

900 g/2 lb mixed green beans, such as broad (fava) beans, French (green) beans, runner beans	vegetarian margarine	6 tbsp single (light) cream
	4 tsp plain (all-purpose) flour	3 tbsp chopped mixed herbs
	300 ml/¹/₂ pint/1 ¹/₄ cups vegetable stock	2 tbsp lemon juice
65 g/2¹/₂ oz/¹/₂ cup butter or	85 ml/3 fl oz dry white wine	rind of 1 lemon
		salt and pepper

1 Cook the beans in a saucepan of boiling salted water for 10 minutes or until tender. Drain and place in a warm serving dish.

2 Meanwhile, melt the butter in a saucepan. Add the flour and cook for 1 minute. Remove the pan from the heat and gradually stir in the stock and wine. Return the pan to the heat and bring to the boil.

3 Remove the pan from the heat once again and stir in the single (light) cream, mixed herbs, lemon juice and zest. Season with salt and pepper to taste. Pour the sauce over the beans, mixing well. Serve immediately.

COOK'S TIP

Use a wide variety of herbs for flavour, such as rosemary, thyme, tarragon and sage.

VARIATION

Use lime rind and juice instead of lemon for an alternative citrus flavour. Replace the single (light) cream with natural (unsweetened) yogurt for a healthier version of this dish.

Curried Cauliflower & Spinach

Serves 4

INGREDIENTS

1 medium cauliflower	1 onion, halved and sliced	salt and pepper
6 tbsp vegetable oil	1 green chilli, sliced	coriander (cilantro) sprigs,
1 tsp mustard seeds	450 g/1 lb spinach	to garnish
1 tsp ground cumin	85 ml/3 fl oz/6 tbsp	
1 tsp garam masala	vegetable stock	
1 tsp turmeric	1 tbsp chopped coriander	
2 garlic cloves, crushed	(cilantro)	

1 Break the cauliflower into small florets.

2 Heat the oil in a deep flameproof casserole dish. Add the mustard seeds and cook until they begin to pop.

3 Stir in the remaining spices, the garlic, onion and chilli and cook for 2–3 minutes, stirring.

4 Add the cauliflower, spinach, vegetable stock, coriander (cilantro) and seasoning and cook over a gentle heat for 15 minutes or until the cauliflower is tender. Uncover the dish and boil for 1 minute to thicken the juices. Garnish and serve.

COOK'S TIP

Mustard seeds are used throughout India and are particularly popular in southern vegetarian cooking. They are fried in oil first to bring out their flavour before the other ingredients are added.

Aubergine (Eggplant) & Courgette (Zucchini) Galette

Serves 4

INGREDIENTS

2 large aubergines (eggplants), sliced	2 tbsp tomato purée (paste)	olive oil, for frying
4 courgettes (zucchini)	2 garlic cloves, crushed	225 g/8 oz Mozzarella cheese, sliced
2 x 400 g/14 oz cans chopped tomatoes, drained	50 m¹/₂ fl oz/4 tbsp olive oil	salt and pepper
	1 tsp caster (superfine) sugar	fresh basil leaves, to garnish
	2 tbsp chopped basil	

1 Put the aubergine (eggplant) slices in a colander and sprinkle with salt. Leave to stand for 30 minutes, then rinse well under cold water and drain. Thinly slice the courgettes (zucchini).

2 Meanwhile, put the tomatoes, tomato purée (paste), garlic, olive oil, sugar and chopped basil into a pan and simmer for 20 minutes or until reduced by half. Season well.

3 Heat 2 tablespoons of olive oil in a large frying pan (skillet) and cook the aubergine (eggplant) slices for 2–3 minutes until just beginning to brown. Remove from the pan.

4 Add a further 2 tablespoons of oil to the pan and fry the courgette (zucchini) slices until browned.

5 Lay half of the aubergine (eggplant) slices in the base of an ovenproof dish. Top with half of the tomato sauce and the courgettes (zucchini) and then half of the Mozzarella.

6 Repeat the layers and bake in a preheated oven, 180°C/350°F/Gas Mark 4, for 45–50 minutes or until the vegetables are tender. Garnish with basil leaves and serve.

Baked Celery with Cream & Pecans

Serves 4

INGREDIENTS

1 head of celery	nut halves	(whole wheat) breadcrumbs
¹/₂ tsp ground cumin	150 ml/¹/₄ pint/²/₃ cup	25 g/1 oz/¹/₄ cup Parmesan
¹/₂ tsp ground coriander	vegetable stock	cheese, grated
1 garlic clove, crushed	150 ml/ ¹/₄ pint/²/₃ cup single	salt and pepper
1 red onion, thinly sliced	(light) cream	celery leaves, to garnish
50 g/1³/₄ oz/¹/₂ cup pecan	50 g/1³/₄ oz fresh wholemeal	

1 Trim the celery and cut into matchsticks. Place the celery in an ovenproof dish with the ground cumin, coriander, garlic, onion and pecan nuts.

2 Mix the stock and cream together and pour over the vegetables. Season with salt and pepper to taste.

3 Mix the breadcrumbs and cheese together and sprinkle over the top to cover the vegetables.

4 Cook in a preheated oven, 200°C/400°F/ Gas Mark 6, for 40 minutes or until the vegetables are tender and the top crispy. Garnish with celery leaves and serve at once.

COOK'S TIP

Once grated, Parmesan cheese quickly loses its 'bite' so it is best to grate only the amount you need for the recipe. Wrap the rest tightly in foil and it will keep for several months in the refrigerator.

VARIATION

You could use carrots or courgettes (zucchini) instead of the celery, if you prefer.

Pepperonata

Serves 4

INGREDIENTS

4 tbsp olive oil

1 onion, halved and finely sliced

2 red (bell) peppers, cut
  into strips

2 green (bell) peppers, cut
  into strips

2 yellow (bell) peppers, cut
  into strips

2 garlic cloves, crushed

2 x 400 g/14 oz cans chopped
  tomatoes, drained

2 tbsp chopped coriander
  (cilantro)

2 tbsp chopped pitted
  black olives

salt and pepper

1 Heat the oil in a large frying pan (skillet). Add the onion and sauté for 5 minutes, stirring until just beginning to colour.

2 Add the (bell) peppers and garlic to the pan and cook for a further 3–4 minutes.

3 Stir in the tomatoes and coriander (cilantro) and season with salt and pepper. Cover the pan and cook the vegetables gently for about 30 minutes or until the mixture is dry.

4 Stir in the pitted black olives and serve the pepperonata immediately.

VARIATION

If you don't like the distinctive flavour of fresh coriander (cilantro), you can substitute it with 2 tbsp chopped fresh flat-leaf parsley. Use green olives instead of black ones, if you prefer.

COOK'S TIP

Stir the vegetables occasionally during the 30 minutes cooking time to prevent them sticking to the bottom of the pan. If the liquid has not evaporated by the end of the cooking time, remove the lid and boil rapidly until the dish is dry.

Souffléd Cheesy Potato Fries

Serves 4

INGREDIENTS

900 g/2 lb potatoes, cut into
    chunks
150 ml/ ¼ pint/ ⅔ cup double
    (heavy) cream
75 g/2¾ oz/¾ cup Gruyère

cheese, grated
pinch of cayenne pepper
2 egg whites
oil, for deep-frying
salt and pepper

chopped flat-leaf parsley and
    grated vegetarian cheese,
    to garnish

1 Cook the potatoes in a saucepan of boiling salted water for 10 minutes. Drain well and pat dry with absorbent paper towels. Set aside until required.

2 Mix the double (heavy) cream and Gruyère cheese in a large bowl. Stir in the cayenne pepper and season with salt and pepper to taste.

3 Whisk the egg whites until stiff peaks form. Fold into the cheese mixture until fully incorporated.

4 Add the cooked potatoes, turning to coat thoroughly in the mixture.

5 Heat the oil for deep-frying to 180°C/350°F or until a cube of bread browns in 30 seconds. Remove the potatoes from the cheese mixture with a slotted spoon and cook in the oil, in batches, for 3–4 minutes or until golden.

6 Transfer the potatoes to a serving dish and garnish with parsley and grated cheese. Serve.

VARIATION

Add other flavourings, such as grated nutmeg or curry powder, to the cream and cheese.

Bulgur Pilau

Serves 4

INGREDIENTS

75 g/2³/₄ oz/6 tbsp butter or
vegetarian margarine
1 red onion, halved and sliced
2 garlic cloves, crushed
350 g/12 oz/2 cups bulgur wheat
175 g/6 oz tomatoes, seeded
and chopped
50 g/1³/₄ oz baby corn cobs,

halved lengthwise
75 g/2³/₄ oz small
broccoli florets
850 ml/1¹/₂ pints/3³/₄ cups
vegetable stock
2 tbsp clear honey
50 g/1³/₄ oz/¹/₃ cup sultanas
(golden raisins)

50 g/1³/₄ oz/¹/₃ cup pine
kernels (nuts)
¹/₂ tsp ground cinnamon
¹/₂ tsp ground cumin
salt and pepper
sliced spring onions (scallions),
to garnish

1 Melt the butter or margarine in a large flameproof casserole dish.

2 Add the onion and garlic and sauté for 2–3 minutes, stirring occasionally.

3 Add the bulgur wheat, tomatoes, corn cobs, broccoli and stock and bring to the boil. Reduce the heat, cover and cook for 15–20 minutes, stirring occasionally

4 Stir in the honey, sultanas (golden raisins), pine kernels (nuts), ground cinnamon, cumin and salt and pepper to taste, mixing well. Remove the casserole from the heat, cover and leave for 10 minutes.

5 Spoon the bulgur pilau into a warm serving dish.

6 Garnish the bulgur pilau with sliced spring onions (scallions) and serve immediately.

COOK'S TIP

The dish is left to stand for 10 minutes in order for the bulgur to finish cooking and the flavours to mingle.

Pesto Potatoes

Serves 4

INGREDIENTS

900 g/2 lb small new potatoes
75 g/2¾ oz/½ cup fresh basil
2 tbsp pine kernels (nuts)
3 garlic cloves, crushed

100 ml/3½ fl oz/½ cup
olive oil
75 g/2¾ oz/¾ cup freshly grated
Parmesan cheese and

Pecorino cheese, mixed
salt and pepper
fresh basil sprigs, to garnish

1 Cook the potatoes in a saucepan of boiling salted water for 15 minutes or until tender. Drain well, transfer to a warm serving dish and keep warm until required.

2 Meanwhile, put the basil, pine kernels (nuts), garlic and a little salt and pepper to taste in a food processor. Blend for 30 seconds, adding the oil gradually, until smooth.

3 Remove the mixture from the food processor and place in a mixing bowl. Stir in the grated Parmesan and Pecorino cheeses.

4 Spoon the pesto sauce over the potatoes and mix well. Garnish with fresh basil sprigs and serve immediately.

COOK'S TIP

This sauce would also make a great dressing for a crisp green salad.

COOK'S TIP

Store this pesto sauce in an airtight container for up to a week in the refrigerator. It can also be frozen (before adding the cheeses) for several months.

Carrot, Orange & Poppy Seed Bake

Serves 4

INGREDIENTS

675 g/1½ lb carrots, cut
into thin strips
1 leek, sliced
300 ml/½ pint/1¼ cups fresh
orange juice

2 tbsp clear honey
1 garlic clove, crushed
1 tsp mixed spice
2 tsp chopped thyme
1 tbsp poppy seeds

salt and pepper
fresh thyme sprigs and orange
rind, to garnish

1 Cook the carrots and leek in a saucepan of boiling salted water for 5–6 minutes. Drain well and transfer to a shallow baking dish until required.

2 Mix together the orange juice, honey, garlic, mixed spice and thyme and pour the mixture over the vegetables. Add salt and pepper to taste.

3 Cover the baking dish and cook in a preheated oven, 180°C/350°F/ Gas Mark 4,

for 30 minutes or until the vegetables are tender.

4 Remove the lid and sprinkle with poppy seeds. Garnish with fresh thyme sprigs and orange rind and serve.

VARIATION

If you prefer, use 2 tsp cumin instead of the mixed spice and omit the thyme, as cumin works particularly well with carrots.

COOK'S TIP

Lemon or lime juice could be used instead of the orange juice if you prefer. Garnish with lemon or lime rind.

Greek Green Beans

Serves 4

INGREDIENTS

400 g/14 oz can haricot (navy)
   beans, drained
1 tbsp olive oil
3 garlic cloves, crushed
425 ml/³/₄ pint/2 cups

vegetable stock
1 bay leaf
2 sprigs oregano
1 tbsp tomato purée (paste)
juice of 1 lemon

1 small red onion, chopped
25 g/1 oz /1¹/₄ cup pitted black
   olives, halved
salt and pepper

1 Put the haricot (navy)
   beans in a flameproof
casserole dish.

2 Add the olive oil and
   crushed garlic and
cook over a gentle heat,
stirring occasionally, for
4–5 minutes.

3 Add the stock, bay leaf,
   oregano, tomato purée
(paste), lemon juice and red
onion, cover and simmer
for about 1 hour or until
the sauce has thickened.

4 Stir in the olives,
   season with salt and
pepper to taste and serve.

COOK'S TIP

*This dish may be made in
advance and served cold
with crusty bread,
if preferred.*

VARIATION

*You can substitute other
canned beans for the haricot
(navy) beans – try
cannellini or black-eyed
beans (peas), or chick-peas
(garbanzo beans) instead.
Remember to drain and
rinse them thoroughly before
use as canned beans often
have sugar or salt added.*

Sweet & Sour Aubergines (Eggplant)

Serves 4

INGREDIENTS

2 large aubergines (eggplant)	seeded and chopped	2 tbsp red wine vinegar
6 tbsp olive oil	3 tbsp chopped mint	1 tsp chilli flakes
4 garlic cloves, crushed	150 ml/ ¼ pint/⅔ cup	salt and pepper
1 onion, cut into eight	vegetable stock	fresh mint sprigs, to garnish
4 large tomatoes,	4 tsp brown sugar	

1 Using a sharp knife, cut the aubergines (eggplant) into cubes. Put them in a colander, sprinkle with salt and leave to stand for 30 minutes. Rinse thoroughly under cold running water and drain well. This process removes all the bitter juices from the aubergines (eggplant). Pat dry with absorbent paper towels.

2 Heat the oil in a large frying pan (skillet) and sauté the aubergine (eggplant), stirring constantly for 1–2 minutes.

3 Stir in the garlic and onion and cook for a further 2–3 minutes.

4 Stir in the tomatoes, mint and stock, cover and cook for 15–20 minutes or until the vegetables are tender.

5 Stir in the brown sugar, red wine vinegar and chilli flakes, season with salt and pepper to taste and cook for 2–3 minutes. Garnish the aubergines with fresh mint sprigs and serve.

COOK'S TIP

Mint is a popular herb in Middle Eastern cooking. It is a useful herb to grow yourself as it can be added to a variety of dishes, particularly salads and vegetable dishes. It can be grown easily in a garden or window box.

Mini Vegetable Puff Pastry Cases

Serves 4

INGREDIENTS

450 g/1 lb puff pastry	spears	1 tsp lime juice
1 egg, beaten	2 tbsp butter or vegetarian	1 tsp chopped thyme
	margarine	pinch of dried mustard
FILLING:	1 leek, sliced	salt and pepper
225 g/8 oz sweet potato, cubed	2 small open-cap mushrooms,	
100 g/3½ oz baby asparagus	sliced	

1 Cut the pastry into 4 equal pieces. Roll each piece out on a lightly floured surface to form a 12.5 cm/5 inch square. Place on a dampened baking tray (cookie sheet) and score a smaller 7.5 cm/ 2.5 inch square inside.

2 Brush with beaten egg and cook in a preheated oven, 200°C/ 400°F/Gas Mark 6, for 20 minutes or until risen and golden brown.

3 Remove the pastry squares from the oven, then carefully cut out the central square of pastry, lift out and reserve.

4 To make the filling, cook the sweet potato in a saucepan of boiling water for 15 minutes, then drain well. Blanch the asparagus in a saucepan of boiling water for 10 minutes or until tender. Drain and reserve.

5 Melt the butter or margarine in a saucepan and sauté the leek and mushrooms for 2–3 minutes. Add the lime juice, thyme and mustard, season well and stir in the sweet potatoes and asparagus. Spoon into the pastry cases, top with the reserved pastry squares and serve immediately.

COOK'S TIP

Use a colourful selection of any vegetables you have at hand for this recipe.

Aubergine (Eggplant) Salad

Serves 4

INGREDIENTS

1 large aubergine (eggplant)	pinch of paprika	GARNISH:
3 tbsp tahini paste	1 tbsp chopped coriander	strips of pimiento
(sesame seed paste)	(cilantro)	lemon wedges
juice and rind of 1 lemon	salt and pepper	toasted sesame seeds
1 garlic clove, crushed	little Gem lettuce leaves	

1 Cut the aubergine (eggplant) in half, place in a colander and sprinkle with salt. Leave to stand for 30 minutes, rinse under cold running water and drain well. Pat dry with paper towels.

2 Place the aubergine (eggplant) halves, skin-side uppermost, on an oiled baking tray (cookie sheet). Cook in a preheated oven, 230°C/450°F/ Gas Mark 8, for 10–15 minutes. Remove from the oven and allow to cool.

3 Cut the aubergine (eggplant) into cubes and set aside until required. Mix the tahini paste (sesame seed paste), lemon juice and rind, garlic, paprika and coriander (cilantro) together. Season to taste and stir in the aubergine (eggplant).

4 Line a serving dish with lettuce leaves and spoon the aubergine (eggplant) into the centre. Garnish the salad with pimiento slices, lemon wedges and toasted sesame seeds and serve.

COOK'S TIP

Tahini paste (sesame seed paste) is a nutty-flavoured sauce available from most health food shops. It is good served with many Middle Eastern dishes.

Salad with Garlic & Yogurt Dressing

Serves 4

INGREDIENTS

75 g/2¾ oz cucumber,
  cut into sticks
6 spring onions (scallions),
  halved
2 tomatoes, seeded
  and cut into eight

1 yellow (bell) pepper, cut into
  strips
2 celery sticks, cut into strips
4 radishes, quartered
75 g/2¾ oz rocket (arugula)
1 tbsp chopped mint, to serve

DRESSING:
2 tbsp lemon juice
1 garlic clove, crushed
150 ml/ ¼ pint/⅔ cup natural
  (unsweetened) yogurt
2 tbsp olive oil
salt and pepper

1 Mix the cucumber, spring onions (scallions), tomatoes, (bell) pepper, celery, radishes and rocket (arugula) together in a large serving bowl.

2 To make the dressing, stir the lemon juice, garlic, natural (unsweetened) yogurt and olive oil together. Season well with salt and pepper.

3 Spoon the dressing over the salad and toss to mix.

4 Sprinkle the salad with chopped mint and serve.

COOK'S TIP

Do not toss the dressing into the salad until just before serving, otherwise it will turn soggy.

COOK'S TIP

Rocket (arugula) has a distinct warm, peppery flavour which is ideal in green salads. Once you have grown it in your garden or greenhouse you will always have plenty as it re-seeds all over the place! If rocket (arugula) is unavailable, lamb's lettuce (corn salad) makes a good substitute.

Courgette (Zucchini), Yogurt & Mint Salad

Serves 4

INGREDIENTS

2 courgettes (zucchini), cut
    into sticks
100 g/3½ oz French (green)
    beans, cut into three
1 green (bell) pepper, cut
    into strips

2 celery sticks, sliced
1 bunch watercress

DRESSING:
200 ml/7 fl oz/¾ cup natural
    (unsweetened) yogurt

1 garlic clove, crushed
2 tbsp chopped mint
pepper

1 Cook the courgettes (zucchini) and French (green) beans in a saucepan of salted boiling water for 7–8 minutes. Drain and leave to cool completely.

2 Mix the courgettes (zucchini) and French (green) beans with the (bell) pepper, celery and watercress in a large bowl.

3 To make the dressing, mix together the natural (unsweetened) yogurt, garlic and chopped mint in a bowl. Season with pepper to taste.

4 Spoon the dressing on to the salad and serve immediately.

COOK'S TIP

The salad must be served as soon as the yogurt dressing has been added – the dressing will start to separate if kept for any length of time.

COOK'S TIP

Watercress is available all year round. Its fresh peppery flavour makes it a delicious addition to many salads.

Bean, Avocado & Tomato Salad

Serves 4

INGREDIENTS

lollo rosso lettuce	175 g/6 oz/2 cups mixed canned	2 tbsp garlic wine vinegar
2 ripe avocados	beans, drained	pinch of caster (superfine) sugar
2 tsp lemon juice	DRESSING:	pinch of chilli powder
4 medium tomatoes	4 tbsp olive oil	1 tbsp chopped parsley
1 onion	drop of chilli oil	

1 Line a serving bowl with the lettuce.

2 Using a sharp knife, thinly slice the avocados and sprinkle with the lemon juice.

3 Thinly slice the tomato and onion. Arrange the avocado, tomatoes and onion around the salad bowl, leaving a space in the centre.

4 Spoon the beans into the centre of the salad and whisk the dressing ingredients together. Pour the dressing over the salad and serve.

COOK'S TIP

Instead of whisking the dressing, place all the ingredients in a screw-top jar and shake vigorously. Any leftover dressing can then be kept and stored in the same jar.

COOK'S TIP

The lemon juice is sprinkled on to the avocados to prevent discoloration when in contact with the air. For this reason the salad should be prepared, assembled and served quite quickly.

Gado Gado

Serves 4

INGREDIENTS

100 g/3$\frac{1}{2}$ oz/1 cup white
   cabbage, shredded
100 g/3$\frac{1}{2}$ oz French (green)
   beans, cut into 3
100 g/3$\frac{1}{2}$ oz carrots, cut into
   matchsticks
100 g/3$\frac{1}{2}$ oz cauliflower florets
100 g/3$\frac{1}{2}$ oz bean sprouts

DRESSING:
100 ml/3$\frac{1}{2}$ fl oz/$\frac{1}{2}$ cup
   vegetable oil
100 g/3$\frac{1}{2}$ oz/1 cup unsalted
   peanuts
2 garlic cloves, crushed
1 small onion, finely chopped
$\frac{1}{2}$ tsp chilli powder
$\frac{1}{3}$ tsp light brown sugar

425 ml/$\frac{3}{4}$ pint/2 cups water
juice of $\frac{1}{2}$ lemon
salt
sliced spring onions (scallions),
   to garnish

1 Cook the vegetables separately in a saucepan of salted boiling water for 4–5 minutes, drain well and chill.

2 To make the dressing, heat the oil in a frying pan (skillet) and fry the peanuts for 3–4 minutes, turning.

3 Remove from the pan with a slotted spoon and leave to drain on absorbent paper towels. Grind the peanuts in a blender or crush with a rolling pin until a fine mixture is formed.

4 Pour all but 1 tbsp oil from the pan and fry the garlic and onion for 1 minute. Add the chilli powder, sugar, a pinch of salt and the water and bring to the boil.

5 Stir in the peanuts. Reduce the heat and simmer for 4–5 minutes until the sauce thickens. Add the lemon juice and leave to cool.

6 Arrange the vegetables in a serving dish and spoon the peanut dressing into the centre. Garnish and serve.

Grilled (Broiled) Vegetable Salad with Mustard Dressing

Serves 4

INGREDIENTS

1 courgette (zucchini), sliced
1 yellow (bell) pepper, sliced
1 aubergine (eggplant), sliced
1 fennel bulb, cut into eight
1 red onion, cut into eight
16 cherry tomatoes
3 tbsp olive oil

1 garlic clove, crushed
fresh rosemary sprigs, to garnish

DRESSING:
4 tbsp olive oil
2 tbsp balsamic vinegar
2 tsp chopped rosemary
1 tsp Dijon mustard
1 tsp clear honey
2 tsp lemon juice

1 Put all of the vegetables except for the cherry tomatoes on to a baking tray (cookie sheet).

2 Mix the oil and garlic and brush over the vegetables. Cook under a medium-hot grill (broiler) for 10 minutes until tender and beginning to char. Leave to cool. Spoon the vegetables into a serving bowl.

3 Mix the dressing ingredients and pour over the vegetables. Cover and chill for 1 hour. Garnish and serve.

COOK'S TIP

This dish could also be served warm – heat the dressing in a pan and then toss into the vegetables.

COOK'S TIP

Balsamic vinegar is made in and around Modena in Italy. It is dark and mellow with a sweet-sour flavour. Although it is rather expensive, you only need a small amount to give a wonderful taste to the dressing. If it is unavailable, use sherry vinegar or white wine vinegar instead.

Red Cabbage & Pear Salad

Serves 4

INGREDIENTS

350 g/12 oz/4 cups red cabbage,
    finely shredded
2 Conference pears,
    thinly sliced
4 spring onions (scallions), sliced
1 carrot, grated

fresh chives, to garnish
lollo biondo leaves, to serve

DRESSING:
4 tbsp pear juice
1 tsp wholegrain mustard
3 tbsp olive oil
1 tbsp garlic wine vinegar
1 tbsp chopped chives

1 Toss the cabbage, pears and spring onions (scallions) together in a bowl.

2 Line a serving dish with lettuce leaves and spoon the cabbage and pear mixture into the centre.

3 Sprinkle the carrot into the centre of the cabbage to form a domed pile.

4 To make the dressing, mix together the pear juice, wholegrain mustard, olive oil, garlic wine vinegar and chives.

5 Pour the dressing over the salad, garnish and serve immediately.

COOK'S TIP

Mix the salad just before serving to prevent the colour from the red cabbage bleeding into the other ingredients.

VARIATION

Experiment with different types of salad leaves. The slightly bitter flavour of chicory (endive) or radicchio would work well with the sweetness of the pears.

Alfalfa, Beetroot & Spinach Salad

Serves 4

INGREDIENTS

100 g/3½ oz baby spinach	DRESSING:	2 tsp clear honey
75 g/2¾ oz alfalfa sprouts	4 tbsp olive oil	1 tbsp chopped chives
2 celery sticks, sliced	1½ tbsp garlic wine vinegar	
4 cooked beetroot, cut into eight	1 garlic clove, crushed	

1 Place the spinach and alfalfa sprouts in a large bowl and mix together.

2 Add the celery and mix well.

3 Toss in the beetroot and mix well.

4 To make the dressing, mix the oil, wine vinegar, garlic, honey and chopped chives.

5 Pour the dressing over the salad, toss well and serve immediately.

COOK'S TIP

If the spinach leaves are too large, tear them up rather than cutting them because cutting bruises the leaves.

COOK'S TIP

Alfalfa sprouts should be available from most supermarkets, if not, use bean sprouts instead.

VARIATION

Add the segments of 1 large orange to the salad to make it even more colourful and refreshing. Replace the garlic wine vinegar with a different flavoured oil such as chilli or herb, if you prefer.

Desserts

Vegetarian or not, confirmed pudding lovers feel a meal is lacking if there isn't a tempting dessert to finish off with. Desserts help to satisfy a deep-seated desire for something sweet and they make us feel good. However, they are often loaded with fat and sugar which are notorious for piling on the calories. Some of the recipes in this chapter offer the perfect solution – they are light, but full of flavour, so you can still enjoy that sweet treat without the bulging waistline!

This chapter contains a wonderful selection of irresistible desserts, perfect for rounding off a meal. There are simple fruit fools that are quick to make, cakes, exotic fruit tarts and all time favourites, such as chocolate cheesecake and steamed sponges. As mentioned in the introduction, vegetarian alternatives may be used for cream and milk in the recipes, and vegetarian gelatine (gelozone) has been used in those recipes that require setting. So take your pick and dip into a delicious dessert!

Raspberry Fool

Serves 4

INGREDIENTS

300 g/10½ oz/1¾ cups fresh
   raspberries
50 g/1¾ oz/ ¼ cup icing
   (confectioners') sugar

300 ml/½ pint/1¼ cups crème
   fraîche, plus extra to
   decorate
½ tsp vanilla essence (extract)

2 egg whites
raspberries and lemon
   balm leaves, to decorate

1 Put the raspberries and icing (confectioners') sugar in a food processor or blender and blend until smooth.

2 Reserve 1 tablespoon per portion of crème fraîche for decorating.

3 Put the vanilla essence (extract) and crème fraîche in a bowl and stir in the raspberry mixture.

4 Whisk the egg whites in a separate mixing bowl until stiff peaks form. Fold the egg whites into the raspberry mixture

using a metal spoon, until fully incorporated.

5 Spoon the raspberry fool into serving dishes and chill for at least 1 hour. Decorate with the reserved crème fraîche, raspberries and lemon balm leaves and serve.

COOK'S TIP

Crème fraîche is usually vegetarian, however, low-fat versions tend to contain gelatine so remember to read the label first.

COOK'S TIP

Although this dessert is best made with fresh raspberries in season, an acceptable result can be achieved with frozen raspberries, which are available from most supermarkets.

VARIATION

This recipe is also delicious made with strawberries or blackberries.

Chocolate Mousse

Serves 8

INGREDIENTS

100 g/3½ oz dark chocolate, melted	4 tbsp caster (superfine) sugar	2 large egg whites
300 ml/½ pint/1¼ cups natural (unsweetened) yogurt	1 tbsp orange juice	coarsely grated dark and white chocolate and orange zest,
150 ml/¼ pint/⅔ cup quark	1 tbsp brandy	to decorate
	1½ tsp gelozone	
	9 tbsp cold water	

1 Put the melted chocolate, natural (unsweetened) yogurt, quark, caster (superfine) sugar, orange juice and brandy in a food processor and blend for 30 seconds. Transfer the mixture to a large bowl.

2 Sprinkle the gelozone over the water and stir until dissolved.

3 In a small saucepan, bring the gelozone and water to the boil for 2 minutes. Leave to cool slightly, then stir into the chocolate mixture.

4 Whisk the egg whites until stiff peaks form and fold into the chocolate mixture using a metal spoon.

5 Line a 850 ml/1½ pint loaf tin (pan) with cling film (plastic wrap). Spoon the mousse into the tin (pan). Chill for 2 hours in the refrigerator until set. Turn the mousse out on to a plate, decorate and serve.

COOK'S TIP

For a quick fruit sauce, blend a can of mandarin segments in natural juice in a food processor and press through a sieve. Stir in 1 tbsp clear honey and serve with the mousse.

Berry Cheesecake

Serves 8

INGREDIENTS

BASE:

75 g/2¾ oz/6 tbsp vegetarian
   margarine

175 g/6 oz oatmeal biscuits

50 g/1¾ oz/¾ cup desiccated
   (shredded) coconut

TOPPING:

1½ tsp gelozone

9 tbsp cold water

125 ml/4 fl oz/½ cup
   evaporated milk

1 egg

6 tbsp light brown sugar

450 g/1 lb/2 cups soft
   cream cheese

350 g/12 oz/1¾ cups
   mixed berries

2 tbsp clear honey

1 Put the margarine in a saucepan and heat until melted. Put the biscuits in a food processor and blend until smooth or crush finely with a rolling pin. Stir into the margarine with the coconut.

2 Press the mixture into a base-lined 20 cm/8 inch spring-form tin (pan) and chill whilst preparing the filling.

3 To make the topping, sprinkle the gelozone

over the water and stir to dissolve. Bring to the boil and boil for 2 minutes. Let cool slightly.

4 Put the milk, egg, sugar and soft cream cheese in a bowl and beat until smooth. Stir in 50 g/ 1¾ oz /¼ cup of the berries. Stir in the gelozone in a stream, stirring constantly, until fully incorporated.

5 Spoon the mixture on to the biscuit base and

return to the refrigerator for 2 hours or until set.

6 Remove the cheesecake from the tin (pan) and transfer to a serving plate. Arrange the remaining berries on top of the cheesecake and drizzle the honey over the top. Serve.

COOK'S TIP

Warm the honey slightly to make it runnier and easier to drizzle.

Steamed Coffee Sponge & Sauce

Serves 4

INGREDIENTS

2 tbsp vegetarian margarine
2 tbsp soft brown sugar
2 eggs
50 g/1¾ oz/⅓ cup plain (all-purpose) flour

¾ tsp baking powder
6 tbsp milk
1 tsp coffee flavouring (extract)

SAUCE:
300 ml/½ pint/1¼ cups milk
1 tbsp soft (light) brown sugar
1 tsp cocoa powder
2 tbsp cornflour (cornstarch)

1 Lightly grease a 600 ml/1 pint heatproof pudding basin. Cream the margarine and sugar until light and fluffy and beat in the eggs.

2 Gradually stir in the flour and baking powder and then the milk and coffee flavouring (extract) to make a smooth batter.

3 Spoon the mixture into the prepared pudding basin and cover with a pleated piece of baking parchment and then a pleated piece of foil, securing around the bowl with string. Place in a steamer or large pan and half fill with boiling water. Cover and steam for 1–1¼ hours or until cooked through.

4 To make the sauce, put the milk, soft (light) brown sugar and cocoa powder in a pan and heat until the sugar dissolves. Blend the cornflour (cornstarch) with 4 tablespoons of cold water to make a paste and stir into the pan. Bring to the boil, stirring until thickened. Cook over a gentle heat for 1 minute.

5 Turn the pudding out on to a serving plate and spoon the sauce over the top. Serve.

COOK'S TIP

The pudding is covered with pleated paper and foil to allow it to rise. The foil will react with the steam and must therefore not be placed directly against the pudding.

Fruit Brûlée

Serves 4

INGREDIENTS

4 plums, stoned and sliced	600 ml/1 pint/2½ cups	1 tsp almond essence (extract)
2 cooking apples, peeled and sliced	Greek-style yogurt	75 g/2¾ oz/⅓ cup demerara (brown crystal) sugar
1 tsp ground ginger	2 tbsp icing (confectioners') sugar, sieved	

1 Put the plums and apples in a saucepan with 2 tablespoons of water and cook for 7–10 minutes until tender but not mushy. Leave to cool, then stir in the ginger.

2 Using a slotted spoon, spoon the mixture into the base of a shallow serving dish.

3 Mix together the Greek-style yogurt, icing (confectioners') sugar and almond essence (extract) and spoon on to the fruit, to cover the fruit completely.

4 Sprinkle the demerara (brown crystal) sugar over the top of the yogurt and cook under a hot grill (broiler) for 3–4 minutes or until the sugar has dissolved and formed a crust. Chill in the refrigerator for 1 hour and serve.

VARIATION

You can vary the fruit in this dish, depending on what is in season – try fresh apricots or peaches. Alternatively, use a 400 g/14 oz can of fruit cocktail.

COOK'S TIP

Use any variety of fruit, such as mixed berries or mango pieces, for this dessert, but do not poach them.

Pear Cake

Serves 12

INGREDIENTS

4 pears, peeled and cored

vegetarian margarine, for
greasing

2 tbsp water

200 g/7 oz/1½ cups plain (all-
purpose) flour

2 tsp baking powder

100 g/3½ oz/½ cup soft (light)
brown sugar

4 tbsp milk

2 tbsp clear honey, plus extra
to drizzle

2 tsp ground cinnamon

2 egg whites

1 Grease and line the base of a 20 cm/8 inch cake tin (pan).

2 Put 1 pear in a food processor with the water and blend until almost smooth. Transfer to a mixing bowl.

3 Sieve in the plain (all-purpose) flour and baking powder. Beat in the sugar, milk, honey and cinnamon and mix well with your fingers.

4 Chop all but one of the remaining pears and add to the mixture.

5 Whisk the egg whites until peaking and gently fold into the mixture until fully blended.

6 Slice the remaining pear and arrange in a fan pattern on the base of the tin (pan).

7 Spoon the cake mixture into the tin (pan) and cook in a preheated oven, 150°C/300°F/Gas Mark 2, for 1¼–1½ hours or until cooked through.

8 Remove the cake from the oven and leave to cool in the tin (pan) for 10 minutes.

9 Turn the cake out on to a wire cooling rack and drizzle with honey. Leave to cool completely, then cut into slices to serve.

Fruit & Nut Loaf

Makes 1 Loaf

INGREDIENTS

225 g/8 oz/1³/₄ cups white bread
    flour, plus extra
    for dusting
¹/₂ tsp salt
1 tbsp vegetarian margarine, plus
    extra for greasing
2 tbsp soft (light) brown sugar

100 g/3¹/₂ oz/²/₃ cup sultanas
    (golden raisins)
50 g/1³/₄ oz/¹/₂ cup no-need to
    soak dried apricots, chopped
50 g/1³/₄ oz/¹/₂ cup
    chopped hazelnuts
2 tsp easy-blend dried yeast

6 tbsp orange juice
6 tbsp natural
    (unsweetened) yogurt
2 tbsp sieved apricot jam

1 Sieve the flour and salt into a mixing bowl. Rub in the margarine and stir in the sugar, sultanas (golden raisins), apricots, nuts and yeast.

2 Warm the orange juice in a saucepan but do not allow to boil.

3 Stir the warm orange juice into the flour mixture with the natural (unsweetened) yogurt and bring the mixture together to form a dough.

4 Knead the dough on a lightly floured surface for 5 minutes until smooth and elastic. Shape into a round and place on a lightly greased baking tray (cookie sheet). Cover with a clean tea towel (dish cloth) and leave to rise in a warm place until doubled in size.

5 Cook the loaf in a preheated oven, 220°C/425°F/Gas Mark 7, for 35–40 minutes until cooked through. Transfer to a cooling rack and brush with the apricot jam. Leave to cool before serving.

COOK'S TIP

To test if the loaf is cooked through – tap the base and if it sounds hollow, it's cooked.

VARIATION

You can vary the nuts according to whatever you have at hand – try chopped walnuts or almonds.

Mixed Fruit Crumble

Serves 4

INGREDIENTS

2 mangoes, sliced	1½ tsp ground ginger	175 g/6 oz/1½ cups plain
1 paw paw (papaya), seeded and	100 g/3½ oz/8 tbsp vegetarian	(all-purpose) flour
sliced	margarine	50 g/1¾ oz desiccated
225 g/8 oz fresh pineapple,	100 g/3½ oz/½ cup soft (light)	(shredded) coconut, plus
cubed	brown sugar	extra to decorate

1 Place the fruit in a pan with ½ tsp of the ginger, 25 g/1 oz/2 tbsp of the margarine and 50 g/1¾ oz/¼ cup of the sugar. Cook over a gentle heat for 10 minutes until the fruit softens. Spoon the fruit into the base of a shallow ovenproof dish.

2 Mix the flour and remaining ginger together. Rub in the remaining margarine until the mixture resembles fine breadcrumbs. Stir in the remaining sugar and the

coconut and spoon over the fruit to cover completely.

3 Cook the crumble in a preheated oven at 180°C/350°F/Gas Mark 4 for about 40 minutes or until the top is crisp. Decorate and serve.

VARIATION

Paw-paws (papayas) have an orangey yellow skin and should yield to gentle pressure.

VARIATION

Use other fruits, such as plums, apples or blackberries, as a fruit base and add chopped nuts to the topping instead of the coconut.

Autumn Fruit Bread Pudding

Serves 8

INGREDIENTS

900 g/2 lb/4 cups mixed
blackberries, chopped apples,
chopped pears

150 g/5½ oz/¾ cup soft (light)
brown sugar
1 tsp cinnamon

225 g/8 oz white bread, thinly
sliced, crusts removed

1 Place the fruit in a
large saucepan with
the soft (light) brown
sugar, cinnamon and
100 ml/3½ fl oz of water,
stir and bring to the boil.
Reduce the heat and
simmer for 5–10 minutes
so that the fruits soften but
still hold their shape.

2 Meanwhile, line
the base and sides of a
850 ml/1½ pint pudding
basin with the bread slices,
ensuring that there are no
gaps between the pieces
of bread.

3 Spoon the fruit into
the centre of the

bread-lined bowl and cover
the fruit with the
remaining bread.

4 Place a saucer on top of
the bread and weight it
down. Chill in the
refrigerator overnight.

5 Turn the pudding out
on to a serving plate
and serve immediately.

COOK'S TIP

*Stand the pudding on a
plate when chilling to catch
any juices that run down the
sides of the basin.*

COOK'S TIP

*This pudding would be
delicious served with
vegetarian vanilla ice cream
to counteract the tartness
of the blackberries.*

Apple Fritters & Almond Sauce

Serves 4

INGREDIENTS

100 g/3¹/₂ oz/³/₄ cup plain
    (all-purpose) flour
pinch of salt
¹/₂ tsp ground cinnamon
12 tbsp/³/₄ cup warm water
4 tsp vegetable oil
2 egg whites

2 dessert (eating) apples, peeled
vegetable or sunflower oil, for
    deep-frying
caster (superfine) sugar and
    cinnamon, to decorate

SAUCE:
150 ml/¹/₄ pint/1¹/₄ cups natural
    (unsweetened) yogurt
¹/₂ tsp almond essence (extract)
2 tsp clear honey

1 Sieve the flour and salt into a mixing bowl.

2 Add the cinnamon and mix well. Stir in the water and oil to make a smooth batter.

3 Whisk the egg whites until stiff peaks form and fold into the batter.

4 Using a sharp knife, cut the apples into chunks and dip the pieces of apple into the batter to coat.

5 Heat the oil for deep-frying to 180°C/350°F or until a cube of bread browns in 30 seconds. Fry the apple pieces, in batches, for 3–4 minutes until golden brown and puffy.

6 Remove the apple fritters from the oil with a slotted spoon and leave to drain on absorbent paper towels.

7 Mix the caster (superfine) sugar and cinnamon and sprinkle over the fritters.

8 Mix the sauce ingredients in a serving bowl and serve with the fritters.

VARIATION

Use pieces of banana or pineapple instead of the apple, if you prefer.

Cherry Pancakes

Serves 4

INGREDIENTS

FILLING:
400 g/14 oz can pitted cherries, plus juice
$^1/_2$ tsp almond essence (extract)
$^1/_2$ tsp mixed spice
2 tbsp cornflour (cornstarch)

PANCAKES:
100 g/3$^1/_2$ oz/$^3/_4$ cup plain (all-purpose) flour
pinch of salt
2 tbsp chopped mint
1 egg
300 ml/$^1/_2$ pint/1$^1/_4$ cups milk

vegetable oil, for frying
icing (confectioners' sugar) and toasted flaked (slivered) almonds, to decorate

1 Put the cherries and 300 ml/$^1/_2$ pint/1$^1/_4$ cups of the juice in a pan with the almond essence (extract) and mixed spice. Stir in the cornflour (cornstarch) and bring to the boil, stirring until thickened and clear. Set aside until required.

2 To make the pancakes, sieve the flour into a bowl with the salt. Add the chopped mint and make a well in the centre. Gradually beat in the egg and milk to make a smooth batter.

3 Heat 1 tbsp of oil in an 18 cm/7 inch frying pan (skillet); pour off the oil when hot. Add just enough batter to coat the base of the frying pan (skillet) and cook for 1–2 minutes or until the underside is cooked. Flip the pancake over and cook for 1 minute. Remove from the pan and keep warm. Heat 1 tbsp of the oil in the pan again and repeat to use up all the batter.

4 Spoon a quarter of the cherry filling on to a quarter of each pancake and fold the pancake into a cone shape. Dust with icing (confectioners') sugar and sprinkle the flaked (slivered) almonds over the top. Serve.

VARIATION

Use other fillings, such as gooseberries or blackberries, as an alternative to the cherries.

Lemon & Lime Syllabub

Serves 4

INGREDIENTS

50 g/1³/₄ oz/¹/₄ cup caster (superfine) sugar
grated zest and juice of 1 small lemon

grated zest and juice of 1 small lime
50 ml/2 fl oz/4 tbsp Marsala or medium sherry

300 ml/¹/₂ pint/1¹/₄ cups double (heavy) cream
lime and lemon zest, to decorate

1 Put the sugar, fruit juices and zest and sherry in a bowl, mix well and leave to infuse for 2 hours.

2 Add the cream to the mixture and whisk until it just holds its shape.

3 Spoon the mixture into 4 tall serving glasses and chill in the refrigerator for 2 hours.

4 Decorate with lime and lemon zest and serve.

VARIATION

For an alternative citrus flavour substitute two oranges for the lemon and lime, if you prefer.

COOK'S TIP

Serve with almond biscuits or uncoated florentines. Do not overwhip the cream when adding to the lemon and lime mixture as it may curdle.

COOK'S TIP

Replace the double (heavy) cream with natural (unsweetened) yogurt for a healthier version of this dessert, or use half quantities of both. Whisk the cream before adding to the yogurt.

Banana & Mango Tart

Serves 8

INGREDIENTS

PASTRY:
20 cm/8 inch baked pastry case

FILLING:
2 small ripe bananas
1 mango, sliced
3¹/₂ tbsp cornflour (cornstarch)
50 g/1³/₄ oz/6 tbsp demerara
   (brown crystal) sugar
300 ml/¹/₂ pint/1¹/₄ cups

soya milk
150 ml/¹/₄ pint/²/₃ cup
   coconut milk
1 tsp vanilla essence (extract)
toasted coconut chips,
   to decorate

1 Slice the bananas and arrange half in the baked pastry case with half of the mango pieces.

2 Put the cornflour (cornstarch) and sugar in a saucepan and mix together. Slowly stir in the soya and coconut milks until combined and cook over a low heat, beating until the mixture thickens.

3 Stir in the vanilla essence then pour the mixture over the fruit.

4 Top with the remaining fruit and toasted coconut chips. Chill in the refrigerator for 1 hour before serving.

COOK'S TIP

Coconut chips are available in some supermarkets and most health food shops. It is worth using them as they look much more attractive and are not as sweet as desiccated (shredded) coconut.

COOK'S TIP

Choose mangoes with shiny and unblemished skins. To test whether they are ripe, gently cup the mango in your hand and squeeze gently – the mango should yield slightly to the touch.

Chocolate & Tofu (Bean Curd) Cheesecake

Serves 12

INGREDIENTS

100 g/3½ oz/¾ cup plain (all-purpose) flour	675 g/1½ lb firm tofu (bean curd)	50 g/1¾ oz/6 tbsp cocoa powder, plus extra
100 g/3½ oz/¾ cup ground almonds	175 ml/6 fl oz/¾ cup vegetable oil	to decorate
200 g/7 oz/¾ cup demerara (brown crystal) sugar	125 ml/4 fl oz/½ cup orange juice	2 tsp almond essence (extract) icing (confectioners') sugar and
150 g/5½ oz/10 tbsp vegetarian margarine	175 ml/6 fl oz/¾ cup brandy	Cape gooseberries, to decorate

1 Put the flour, ground almonds and 1 tablespoon of the sugar in a bowl and mix well. Rub the margarine into the mixture to form a dough.

2 Lightly grease and line the base of a 23 cm/9 inch spring-form tin (pan). Press the dough into the base of the tin (pan) to cover, pushing the dough right up to the edge of the tin (pan).

3 Roughly chop the tofu (bean curd) and put in a food processor with all of the remaining ingredients and blend until smooth and creamy. Pour over the base in the tin (pan) and cook in a preheated oven, 160°C/325°F/ Gas Mark 3, for 1–1¼ hours or until set.

4 Leave to cool in the tin (pan) for 5 minutes, then remove from the tin (pan) and chill in the refrigerator. Dust with icing (confectioners') sugar and cocoa powder. Decorate and serve.

Chocolate Fudge Pudding

Serves 4

INGREDIENTS

50 g/1¾ oz/4 tbsp vegetarian
  margarine, plus extra
  for greasing
75 g/2¾ oz/6 tbsp soft light
  brown sugar

2 eggs, beaten
350 ml/12 fl oz/1 ¼ cups milk
50 g/1¾ oz ½ cup chopped
  walnuts

40 g/1½ oz/¼ cup plain
  (all-purpose) flour
2 tbsp cocoa powder
icing (confectioners') sugar and
  cocoa, powder to dust

1 Lightly grease a
1 litre/1¾ pint
ovenproof dish.

2 Cream together the
margarine and sugar
in a large mixing bowl until
fluffy. Beat in the eggs.

3 Gradually stir
in the milk and add
the walnuts.

4 Sieve the flour and
cocoa powder into the
mixture and fold in gently,
with a metal spoon,
until well mixed.

5 Spoon the mixture into
the dish and cook in a
preheated oven at 180°C/
350°F/Gas Mark 4 for
35–40 minutes or until the
sponge is cooked.

6 Dust with icing
(confectioners') sugar
and cocoa powder and serve.

VARIATION

*Add 1–2 tbsp brandy or
rum to the mixture for a
slightly alcoholic pudding, or
1–2 tbsp orange juice for a
child-friendly version.*

COOK'S TIP

*Serve this pudding with
crème fraîche for a
luxuriously rich dessert.*

Index

Index compiled by Lydia Darbyshire